IF
I HAD
A WISH···

by Ethel Barrett

G/L REGAL BOOKS™

A Regal Venture Book
A Division of G/L Publications
Glendale, California, U.S.A.

© Copyright 1974 by G/L Publications

Published by Regal Books Division, G/L Publications
Glendale, California   91209
Printed in U.S.A.

Second Printing, 1976

Library of Congress Catalog Card No. 74-83139
ISBN 0-8307-0314-4

The Scripture versions used in *If I Had a Wish*
include:
King James Version
The Living Bible, Paraphrased (Wheaton:
Tyndale House Publishers, 1971). Used
by permission.

CONTENTS

This book is a delightful resource for teachers and students studying *One Nation Under God* (G/L Bible study Course 54). Available from your church supplier.

Other Regal Venture Books
by Ethel Barrett

The Strangest Thing Happened . . .
Which Way to Nineveh?
The People Who Couldn't Be Stopped
The Secret Sign
Rules—Who Needs Them?
I'm No Hero

These Regal Venture books make Bible stories
come alive for readers of every age. Also,
provide exciting resources for G/L pre-teens
Bible studies.

For Family Bible storytimes
It Didn't Just Happen

THERE ARE
SOME THINGS THAT JUST
HAVE TO GO . . .

Once you start growing up, that is.

This is news to you at first, of course. Each comfortable thing you have to give up comes as a shock. But by the time you've started school and entered organized society, there are a lot of things you've dumped by the wayside. You no longer suck your thumb. Bed wetting is out. And somewhere along the line they've taken away your favorite blanket. The pacifier is gone too, and you can no longer dump your bowl of food upside down over your head.

But there is one thing you can never quite give up.

And that is—wishing.

No matter how much you grow up in other areas, you just can't give up wishing. You have a built-in "wisher" that computes wishes as fast as you feed it the information. You wish for good things, bad things, zany things, unreasonable things, *impossible* things.

1

You wish you were taller, shorter, fatter, thinner, smarter, wittier, richer, more sparkling—

And sometimes you wish you could dent the rules a little, and get away with it. And sometimes you wish *horrible* things about other people—not only your "enemies" but sometimes even those you love the best.

At times you feel guilty about it. "What's the matter with me?" you say. "Here I am, umpty-ump years old, and my computer is still grinding out childish wishes."

News for you. If you live to be a hundred, you'll still be grinding out "childish" wishes. Even though you know that "Wishing Will Make It So"[1] isn't so, that crazy computer just won't turn off.

This book is about wishes and the people who made them. Some of them were good, some of them were not so good, some of them were disastrous. Now these men lived thousands of years ago, but the stories are very much up-to-date. For each story is a story of you. And your own heart. And your own thoughts. And some of the wishes that you might have made yourself.

1. Like in the song.

I WISH
I COULD FIB A LITTLE

"I don't mean I want to tell lies all the time. Actually, I hate liars. And I don't like people to lie to me. But I wish, just once in a while, I could fib and get away with it. Like when I'm backed into a corner, or like when I think I might get hurt if I don't fib, or like when I know I *will* get punished if I don't fib. Some lies do seem harmless. And there are kids all around me who lie all the time and get away with it. They even seem to be happy.

"Yes—and even my mother and dad lie sometimes. I'd never come right out and call them liars because I'd get smacked. But I've heard them lie their way out of tight spots more than once. I wish it were true that you could tell a lie once in a while and it would be okay. I know that bad guys lie all the time. But what about the good guys? Can't a good guy lie—once in a while?"

Of course he can.

"Well—does he get away with it?"

Now that's a very interesting question. And it has some very interesting answers. Let's explore a bit, and find out whether a good guy *does* get away with it.

The lone figure hurried along through the brush, keeping off the main path, as if he did not want to be seen.

Who was he? A prince, perhaps? His clothing looked expensive. His tunic and cloak were of fine wool. But he had no servants with him. He couldn't be a prince—traveling alone. But he certainly must be somebody from the palace; his clothing looked it. Or at least a nobleman's son.

A warrior? No. A closer look would show that he had absolutely no weapons at all. And he had no soldiers with him. Indeed he did not look as if he were going to battle. A shepherd looking for his sheep? No, not possibly—not with those clothes. He didn't even carry a slingshot.

A fugitive? Ah, yes, that was it. He was hurrying. And from the look on his face, he was worrying. And from his furtive[1] looks over his shoulder he was worrying. He was afraid he was being followed. He was sure-footed, like someone who was used to taking care of himself, someone who was used to the wilderness. He walked with grace, not even snapping a twig on his way.

He *was* from the king's palace.

And he was in trouble.

His name was David.

David started out as a shepherd boy.

And he would have lived and died and never been heard of again, except that one day a very astonishing thing happened to him. The great prophet Samuel, no less, had come to his house, and before the astonished eyes of his father and brothers, announced that David was going to be the next

---

1. He didn't want anyone to know he was peeking.

king of Israel. And to show that he meant business, anointed him king then and there.

Now just how all this was going to come about, no one was sure, at the moment.[2] They only knew that it would come about for sure, because God Himself had said so.

And from that moment on, David's life was never to be the same again.

Now if anyone had told David that he would go from being anointed king to something even more astonishing, David wouldn't have believed it. But he did.

He fought a giant!

Israel was at war with the Philistines, and David's father sent him to the battlefield. Not to fight—but to take some food and provisions to his older brothers, who *were* fighting. In those days battles were sometimes settled by choosing a warrior from each side and letting them fight it out. Whoever won, won for his entire army. And his country won the war.

Now the warrior chosen by the Philistines was none other than the giant Goliath. And David? Before he could say, "Where's my sword and my sandals?" *he* was chosen to fight him![3]

Now this in itself was unusual enough—but the most astonishing thing of all was that David killed the rascal!

Then things began to happen at such a dizzy pace—it was enough to turn any poor shepherd boy's head. The crowds cheered and roared and danced and praised David to the skies—

And King Saul got jealous.

From there on out, things went from bad to worse.

The more popular David became with the people, the more jealous King Saul became. He spilled his jealousy all over the palace, too, so that no one there dared to speak well of David above a whisper.

2. King Saul was ruling at the time.
3. You can read all about it in the book, *Rules—Who Needs Them?*

7

David did have one friend in the palace. His name was Jonathan. And Jonathan and David were the closest of friends, closer than brothers, bosom pals, you might say. There was only one little problem.

Jonathan happened to be *King Saul's own son.*

Did this make things better?

No, this made things worse. What? David was in trouble? Yes, David was in trouble.

King Saul had threatened David's life, and that's about the worst kind of trouble you can get into.

David was fleeing for his life.

And so, in our little drama, the characters are:

Saul, the king, who has threatened to kill David.

David, who is running for his life.

Jonathan, Saul's son and David's friend, who helped him escape.

Now, on with the story.

The late afternoon shadows were stretched across the desert. David stopped a minute and shaded his eyes. He'd walked from late in the morning until now. And he was tired. The sweat dribbled off his beard as he looked ahead of him. There, a few miles away was the town of Nob where the priests of Israel lived, where the Tabernacle was, where the sacred Ark of God was kept. It was the center of the nation's worship. And there the priests of Israel lived. Beyond was Jerusalem, way off on the horizon.

But it was not Jerusalem he wanted; it was Nob. He knew the priests of Nob and they knew him. It was his only chance for shelter, his only chance for help. He sighed, and started on toward it. He wouldn't stay there long, he thought—just overnight, perhaps only for a few hours. There he could get some food, perhaps even some weapons. Then he'd be on his way. Where, he did not know.

Ooops. Someone coming to meet him. David stopped and

8

shaded his eyes again. It was Ahimelech (Ah-*him*-eh-lek), the high priest. And he looked worried.

"David! David!" he called out. "What is the matter?"

He *was* worried.

"Ho!" David called out, with as much confidence as he could muster. But there was no cheerful "Ho!" in return.

"Why are you alone, David?" said Ahimelech. "Why is no one with you? Where are your men? Is something wrong?"

He is not just worried, David thought. He is frightened, terribly frightened. Could he have found out that David had run away from Saul? And if he had found out, was he afraid of Saul? Would he be afraid to help David for fear Saul would take it out on him?

David realized that the high priest was waiting for an answer. What could he say? He was in a spot, varnished into a corner, backed against the wall, in a hole, up a tree, in a pickle, and absolutely at his wit's end. Now was the time to act, to be brave, to come out with it, and all sorts of lofty things—but instead—

"I am on a secret mission for the king," he lied.

Now this was a cagey answer. It was an answer calculated to get David out of trouble and to get him help. And it satisfied the high priest. There was only one thing wrong with it.

It wasn't true.

They started walking back toward the town, the servants of the high priest plodding along beside them. "But where are your men?" Ahimelech said.

Now the problem with a lie is that it is seldom able to stand on its own feet. You usually have to tell another lie to prop up the first one.

"Where are your men?" Ahimelech said again. "Surely you brought men with you."

Oh, oh. David's little lie was sagging.

"I—uh—asked them to meet me at—uh—a certain place. It's a secret," he said, dragging out another lie to prop the first one up. "I can't tell you where they are. King Saul told me

9

not to tell anybody why I'm here. I've told my men where to meet me later."

By this time they had entered the town and were standing at the entrance to the Tabernacle. There it was—the center of worship for all of Israel.

"Now," said David, "what is there to eat? Can you give me some bread? Or anything else? Give me whatever you have."

"Well, we don't have any regular bread," Ahimelech said, "but there's the holy bread. We're just ready to change it for five fresh loaves. I can give you that."

"I'll take it," said David. "Is there anything else?"

"That's all there is," said Ahimelech. "What else can I do for you?"

"Do you have a spear I could use," said David, "or a sword? This business of the king's required much haste. I left in such a rush I came away without a weapon."

"Well," said Ahimelech, "I have a sword. It's the sword of Goliath the Philistine. The fellow you killed in the valley of Elah."

"You have *that* sword here?" said David.

"Yes. It's wrapped in a cloth in a closet for safekeeping. Take it if you want it. There's nothing else here. If you can use—"

"I'll take it," said David. "It's just the thing."

Ahimelech gave the orders and his helpers went for the sword. David buckled it on. He glanced at a group of men who were gathering around, as he did so. He had carried it off very well, he thought. They had believed his lies; they weren't suspicious.

"Thank you," he said to Ahimelech. "I'll be on my way. I have to hurry." He patted the sword at his side, gathered up the loaves of bread, and turned and left.

But a little apart from the group, there was a man who was watching him with narrowed eyes.

He wasn't just any onlooker.

His name was Doeg (*Doh*-eg).

And he was one of Saul's chief men—the overseer of all Saul's herdsmen.

There was trouble ahead.

David hurried on to Gath,[4] and from there to Adullam where he lived in a cave, and from *there*, back to Judah. By this time he had collected many followers—including his own family![5]

They just kept coming—those who were in any kind of trouble, and those who were discontented with the king's rule—until finally David was the leader of about four hundred men. Once in Judah, he settled himself and his followers in the forest of Hereth, where everything would have been fine—

Except for one little problem.

A problem by the name of Doeg.

Saul was back in Gibeah when the news reached him. He was sitting under an oak tree, practicing his snurl,[6] and playing a sort of mumbly-peg in the dirt with his spear. He was surrounded by his officers, and from their worried faces, it was easy to see that he was in a very bad mood. David's problem was standing only a few feet away.

Doeg.

"David is *where?*" shouted Saul.

"Right here in Judah, sire," his officers said, "in the forest of Hereth."

"You—you men of Benjamin!" Saul shrieked. "What is this? Is everybody plotting against me? And who is David? Has

---

4. Where they said, "Who needs him? Send him on his way!"
5. He put his parents in Mizpah for safekeeping.
6. A cross between a sneer and a snarl.

he promised you fields and vineyards and commissions in his army?"

"But sire—"

"Is that why you're against me?" Saul bellowed. And then he began to rant and rave about everything that had been bothering him for months. "Not one of you has ever told me that my own son Jonathan is on David's side."

"But sire, your son—"

"You're not even sorry for me!"

"But—"

"Think of it! My own son—encouraging David to come and kill me!"

There was a great silence for a moment. None of it was true, of course. No one knew what to say. The king was raving mad again. But a great unspoken question hung in the air. Who *had* helped David? Who had given him weapons? Who had helped him get away? Who had given him food? Was it someone standing right there among the king's officers? Or was it Jonathan?

"Ahimelech," someone said. "It was Ahimelech."

Everyone turned to see who had spoken. Then one of the officers stepped forward from the rest. "When I was in Nob," he began—

Good grief. It was Doeg!

Saul's bellowing was reduced to a mere sputter.[7] "When I was in Nob," Doeg went on, "I saw David there. Talking to the high priest. He asked for food. And Ahimelech gave him five loaves of bread. They were taking the loaves off the altar; it was time for them to be exchanged for fresh loaves."

"And?" Saul's jaw was sagging. "Go on, go on."

"Then David asked him for a weapon, any weapon. And Ahimelech gave him a sword."

"A sword? From the Tabernacle?"

7. A mini bellow.

"The sword of Goliath, sire. It was there for safekeeping."

There was a great hissing sound, like that of a goose, as Saul let his breath out. And then they watched Saul as he turned from pink to red, to purple, and then to a combination of all three, like a week-old bruise. He looked like a boiler about ready to blow up but when he spoke, his voice was quiet.

"Send for Ahimelech," he said at last. "And all the priests at Nob. Bring them here to me."

The message got through David's security quickly. It was important. "It's Abiathar," they told David, "Ahimelech's son. He wants to see you. He wants to talk to you. He has escaped."

"Escaped?" David said, getting to his feet. "Escaped from what?"

"We're bringing him now to talk to you. He will tell you himself," they said.

Abiathar looked haggard when they brought him up to where David was. David motioned to some of his men to get food and water. "What happened?" he said. "Did your father send you? What's wrong?"

"My father is dead," Abiathar said.

"Dead? What happened?"

"All the priests are killed, and their families and their cattle. The whole town is wiped out."

"King Saul?"

"King Saul. He ordered it done when he found out that you had been there and that my father had helped you. He ordered it done."

"But they were innocent! They were *innocent!*" David cried. "They knew nothing about any trouble between King Saul and me!"

"My father tried to tell them that. That he knew nothing of any plot against Saul; that you had always been faithful. And that he never suspected that there was anything wrong.

13

But the king was mad with rage. He shouted at his bodyguards to kill us all."

"And who did the killing? The soldiers?"

"No. They refused to harm the priests of God."

"Jonathan?" David whispered.

"No, Jonathan wasn't there."

"Then who?"

"It was Doeg. He seemed eager to carry out the king's wishes. He ordered his men to kill the priests. And then they went to Nob and wiped out the town."

David's face was white with shock and horror. "I knew it," he said. "I knew it. When I saw Doeg there, I knew he would tell Saul. But that this would happen—"

David's men had brought refreshment to Abiathar. And they made him sit down and drink and eat and rest. David sat down beside him. "I've caused the death of all your family," he said. "Stay here with me."

Abiathar did not answer. "Stay here with me," David went on, "and I will protect you with my own life. No one will hurt you. I won't allow it." He ordered his men to bring Abiathar his equipment—a weapon, a flask of water, anything he needed.

These good people at Nob had protected him. And now they were dead. They had protected him and they had been killed for doing it. He looked up at Abiathar. "If anyone harms you," he said, "it will be over my dead body."

And he put his head in his hands and wept.

What was ahead? No one knew. They would just have to sit tight and wait.

What Do You Think?

Did David's lie cause all the trouble? Is it possible that the priests would have protected him if David had told them the truth? If you understand *why* a person would tell a lie, does it make the lie right?

One thing you have to say for David, he did not try to

defend himself. He didn't make excuses. It was his fault and he knew it and he admitted it.

He was not only sorry, but he did something about it. He offered to protect Abiathar with his own life. He could not do any more than that.

I WISH
HE WERE DEAD

CHAPTER 2/ 1 Samuel 23; 24

Have you ever said this about someone, or even thought it? If you have, it's a pretty hard thing to admit. Have you ever said, "Oh, drop dead," or even muttered it under your breath? Well, you can't help these thoughts from entering your mind. The trick is to shoo them right out again. Don't invite them in to play around.

These are the thoughts that entered Saul's mind. And Saul's problem was that he *did* invite them in to play around. "I wish he were dead," he muttered to himself a dozen times a day. And the "he" he was thinking of, was David. Until it got to the point where he couldn't even think about David without thinking, "I wish he were dead."

Now Saul had a kingdom to rule. He had a fine family. And a good son—Jonathan. And instead of staying home and ruling his kingdom, he wasted all his energy tracking down David. And so the latter part of his reign became an enormous and foolish game of hide-and-seek. He missed the whole point of the job God had given him to do.

17

Hide

"I'd like to do God's will—if these people would only leave me alone. I can't get anything done that God wants me to do; I keep running from all these problems."

If anybody could have said that, David could. He had one big problem that seemed to fill his whole life. And it was keeping one jump ahead of Saul. He could have just hidden himself in the wilderness and made himself comfortable with his little band of followers and called it quits. But he knew in his heart that God had a job for him to do. He knew that Samuel the prophet had anointed him king. He knew that God had this great plan for his life. And he knew that somehow, someday, there would be a way out of his troubles. He had only to keep his connection with God unbroken.

He had about six hundred followers by now. And he also had a prophet. Yes, Ahimelech's son, Abiathar became David's prophet.[1] And David had intelligence and counter-intelligence just like we have today—he had spies sent out in all directions to let him know what was going on. So when they told him that the Philistines were attacking a little town in Judah called Keilah and robbing the people of their grain, David forgot his own problems and shifted right into his "business as usual" gear.

"Lord, shall I go attack these Philistines?" he asked.[2]

"Yes," said the Lord. "Go and attack them and save Keilah."

Now David was ready to go, but his men had a different opinion. "Oh," they howled and "No," they begged. "We're scared enough right here in Judah. We certainly don't want to go to Keilah and fight the whole Philistine army!"

Was this a sign that God did not want David to go? David checked it out to make sure. "Shall I go?" he asked. And

1. He was a go-between for the king and God.
2. The Bible tells us that God spoke to David through Abiathar.

18

God said, "Yes. I told you. Go down to Keilah. I'll help you conquer the Philistines."

And that's exactly the way it turned out.

Wop! The Philistines were conquered.

Wooooosh! Their cattle were confiscated.[3]

At 'em! The Philistines were put to rout. And the people of Keilah were saved.

But—

—And Seek

Saul's spies were busy. "There's news of David," they told Saul.

"Where is the rascal now?"

"He's at Keilah."

"Keilah? Good! He's in a walled city! It's a ready-made trap! We'll get him for sure!" And he mobilized his whole army to march to Keilah. This time he figured he could say "Gotcha!" for sure. But—

Hide

David's spies were on their toes. Saul was coming with his whole army, they said, and fast. David sent for Abiathar, to ask the Lord what he should do. "Saul is coming to Keilah because I'm here," he said, "and fast. If he catches me here I'll be caught. It's a ready-made trap. Will the men of Keilah surrender me to him? And will Saul actually come, as my spies have told me? Oh, Lord, tell me—I need to know."

"He will come," the Lord said.

"Then I have another question," David said. "Will the men of Keilah betray me to him?"

"Yes," said the Lord. "They will betray you."

"Thank You, Lord," David said to the Lord. And then to his men, "Let's go." And they packed up their duds and left. The Bible tells us they began to roam the country wher-

---

3. Snatched by force; sort of legalized stealing.

ever they could find a place to go. They kept hiding.

—And Seek

"He's gone," Saul's spies told him.

"Where?"

"We don't know. He's wandering in the wilderness. He and his men are staying in caves."

"Drat it," said Saul. "There's no sense going to Keilah now. Just keep me posted. I'll hunt him down, wherever he is."

And Saul did hunt David, day after day. But the Bible tells us the Lord didn't let him find him.

Hide

David was at Horesh when his spies told him again that someone was hunting for him. But this time it was not Saul. When David saw his visitor from a distance he leaped to his feet. They started walking quickly toward each other at first. Then they both broke into a run.

"Jonathan!"

"David!"

The two friends were together at last. They hugged each other for joy. And wept a little, too. "Jonathan, Jonathan," David said, "I thought I'd never see you again."

"Don't be afraid," Jonathan said. "My father will never find you."

"I don't know how much longer I can hold out," David said.

"You'll hold out," Jonathan said. "You're going to be the next king of Israel. God has said so."

"Not if Saul can help it," muttered David.

"My father is well aware that you're going to be king. That's why he's chasing you. That's why he wants you dead. But God is on your side. And I am your friend."

"Sometimes I think you're the only friend I have in the world," David said. "I wish you could stay. But I would not want you to fight against your own father. I know you have to go."

"Yes. I have to go," Jonathan said. "You stay here. And I'll pray that God will keep you safe." Jonathan turned to leave. A few yards away, he turned back and looked at David.

"Go with God," David called.

Jonathan waved. And shook his head yes. And turned away again. A few moments later he was gone. But he had left the warmth of friendship behind, and the glow of unselfish love. "Go with God, Jonathan," David said again under his breath. "And God keep you safe."

—And Seek

"There are some men here to see you, sire," Saul's men told him.

"Who are they?"

"They are men from the country of Ziph."

"Let me talk to them," said Saul, "at once." Perhaps they knew where David was hiding.

They did.

"We know where David is," they said. "He is in the caves of Horesh on Hachilah hill. Down in the southern part of the wilderness."

"Ahhhh," Saul said, stroking his beard. "I've been wishing David dead for so many months. Perhaps this time. Perhaps this time. . . ."

"Come on down," the men said, as if they could read his mind, "and we'll catch him for you. And your fondest wish will be fulfilled."

"Good, good," said Saul. "At last someone has pity on me." They turned to leave. "But wait—" Saul said.

"Yes, sire?"

"Go check again to make sure he's staying and who has seen him there. For he is crafty. He'll slip through your fingers."

"Yes, sire."

"Discover his hiding places, check your facts—and come back and give me a more definite report. And then I'll go with you." He fingered his spear. "And if he's in the area at all, I'll find him. I'll find him if I have to search every inch of the land."

"Yes, sire."

"He's crafty," Saul said again. They turned to leave.

"Very crafty," he muttered.

But they were gone.

Hide

"Saul is on his way here," David's men told him.

"Then we move on again," said David. And they did. Further into the wilderness of Maon in the south of the desert.

But Saul followed them there, wherever they went.

David kept trying to escape. "This way," David would say. And then, *"This* way." And he zigged and he zagged along the side of the mountain. But Saul's men kept closing in. He was practically breathing down David's neck.

Closer they came.

And closer.

"This way." The orders were now given in whispers. "And this way. And this way."

But it was no use. Saul's men were so close, it was dangerous even to snap a twig. Closer they came, and closer. And closer. And then—

A message reached Saul from his home front.

"What is it?" he wanted to know.

"The Philistines!" the messengers said. "They're raiding Israel again. You've got to go back!"

Curses! Just when he had David almost in his hand!

"I can't let him go!" he bellowed. "He's almost in my hand," he wailed. "All I have to do is close my fist! I can't quit the chase! I can't quit now!" But with all his bellowing and all his stomping and all his raging, there was only one thing left for him to do—

Quit the chase.

Phew!

Ever since that time the place where David was camped has been called "The Rock of Escape"!

It was the closest shave till straight razors were invented.

—And Seek

Saul's battle with the Philistines was over. Israel was safe again. He could get his mind back on his fondest wish.

David's death.

"He's gone into the wilderness of En-gedi," Saul's men told him. "Ahh," said Saul, and "AhHAH. This time I'll get him for sure. I won't miss this time. We'll start at once. Three thousand troops."

"Yes, sire."

"*Special* troops!" he cried after them.

"Yes, sire," they said.

And he set out with three thousand specially trained troops toward En-gedi.

Gotcha! The Chase Is Over!

There on the east edge of the desert of Judah lay En-gedi. It seemed to go up and down instead of sideways. There the limestone cliffs towered six hundred feet above the Dead Sea. A huge stream plunged from the top, leaping over the cliffs in waterfalls down to the sea. It looked for all the world like a mountain goat, giving the place the nickname, "Fountain of the Kid." It was riddled with caves, and in front of nearly every cave was a rough stone wall, built there by the shepherds to protect their flocks from wild beasts, and to shelter them from bad weather. The sheep grazed in the grassy spots, and the wild goats climbed the limestone rocks. There were caves aplenty—enough to use for sheep and enough to spare. And some of them were *enormous!*[4]

4. Very, very big! Absolutely huge!

Saul and his men descended on the place like buzzards, making a door-to-door search—only in this place it was a cave-to-cave search. Somewhere, in one of those caves, David and his men had to be hiding.

But no matter how terrible an army is, it is after all made up of human beings. And they had to eat. And they had to rest. And Saul, even though he was the king, was only human too. So at one point in the search, he went into one of the caves. And he took off his outer robe and laid it aside. And sat down.

Wait a minute. Was that a rustle he heard? What was it? Was it voices? Some kind of an animal? Bats, perhaps. Ah, yes, that was it. It was probably bats.

It *was* bats. Or was it?

But he couldn't shake the feeling that what he heard was whispering. And he couldn't shake the eerie[5] feeling that there was another person (or persons?) in the cave. He shivered. Suddenly he wanted to get out of there. He groped in the dark for his robe. He put it over his shoulders hurriedly and groped his way out of the cave, glad to get out in the light again. His guards were waiting for him outside. Suddenly he felt better. In the bright daylight, everything seemed all right again. Why had he been so frightened back in there? He shook off the feeling, and scrambled along the ledge, glad to be on his way.

Now he was the king, the commander again. He started briefing his men, giving them orders. When suddenly—

"My lord the king!"

Saul stopped in his tracks. There it was again.

"My lord the king!"

It couldn't be. But it was.

David!?!

Saul whirled around. It *was* David. Back in the distance. And he was bowing low! Saul gaped at him, his mouth sagging

5. Real spooky.

open, his eyes nearly popping out of his head. He could not answer. He'd lost his tongue.

"Why do you listen to people who say I'm trying to harm you?" David shouted. "Why I could have killed you only a moment ago! The Lord placed you at my mercy. Back in the cave—"

Back there in the cave? *Back there in the cave?!?* Oh, *no!*

"Oh, *yes!*" shouted David, as if he could read Saul's mind. "I was back there in the cave. With my men. And some of my men wanted me to kill you."

Saul still couldn't find his tongue.

"But I spared you," David went on, "for I said, 'I will never harm him; he is the Lord's chosen king.' "

Some of Saul's men took a step forward, but he shushed them with his hand. They stopped stiff, as if they were in the middle of a game of "Statue."

"See what I have in my hand?" David went on. And he waved something in the air. It was a long piece of cloth.

"You don't know what it is?" David cried. "Then I'll tell you what it is! It's the hem of your robe. I cut it off. But I didn't kill you. Will you believe now that I'm not trying to harm you? Yes, in spite of your wickedness, I'll not touch you."

Saul would have sat down if he'd dared. His knees were so wobbly, it was only his willpower that kept him on his feet. Every word of David's was like a blow.

But David wasn't finished yet. "Who is the king trying to catch, anyway? Why do you spend your time chasing *me?* I'm a big nothing! I'm worthless as a flea!"

Saul opened his mouth to speak. And then he closed it again. Suddenly he felt very very tired. And very, very foolish. "May the Lord judge which of us is right," David was saying, "and punish whoever is wrong."

Suddenly all the strength went out of Saul. As big as he was he seemed to shrivel and pucker up like a balloon when someone has slowly let the air out of it. How stupid he'd been to spend all of this time chasing David all over the lot, hating David, wanting to kill David, when he should have been home ruling his kingdom. Here he had spent every waking minute wishing David was dead. And now David had just had a chance to kill *him*—and he hadn't done it.

"Is it really you, my son David?" Saul called out. It was all he could think of to say.

And then he began to cry.

They all stood there, his men and David's men. The only sound was the waterfall in the distance, and Saul, crying. "You're a better man than I am, David," he sobbed. "You've repaid me good for evil. You could have killed me just now. And you didn't. May the Lord reward you for the kindness you've shown me."

He stood there looking at David for a moment, David grown to be a man, standing tall, his feet spread apart, and the hem of Saul's robe in his hand. And he knew in that moment that David was surely going to be king one day.

"When you are king, David," he said at last, "promise me that you will not kill my family."

"I promise," said David quietly. And he stood there still and tall. There was nothing more to say. For at that moment everyone there knew that Saul spoke the truth.

David would be king.

Saul signaled his men to gather their duds and prepare to go home.

David and his men turned to go back to their cave. "You had him right in your hand," his men said. "You could have killed him. And you only slit off the bottom of his robe." David shook his head. "Like I told you back in the cave," he said. "I shouldn't even have done that. No matter what he has done—he is still the king. It's a serious sin to attack God's chosen king in any way."

"But *you* are God's chosen king," his men said.

"Hold it," said David. "Not yet."

26

"And in the meantime?" said his men.

"Tell the men to pack up and get ready to move. In the meantime we just wait."

And let God work this out. His own way.

What Do You Think?

David had come a long way from the young man who told two lies in one breath when he was first running away from Saul. He was going through the school of hard knocks. And he was getting more than just passing grades; he was passing his tests with honors. The more troubles he had, the more of a man he became.

Saul's only thought had been "I wish he were dead." And David, even when he had a chance to kill Saul, thought—"I can't touch him. God is still running the show."

And so they each went their separate ways. But the show wasn't over yet. David continued to hide—and wait for God. And Saul? Well, he was still thinking upside down and backwards.

And there was more trouble ahead.

Remember: "Anyone who hates his Christian brother is really a murderer at heart" (1 John 3:15, *TLB*).

I WISH
I HAD A CHANCE
TO GET EVEN

"Of course I wouldn't just go out and get even on purpose. I mean if a chance to get even was just dumped right into my lap—that would be great. It would give me a lot of satisfaction. I just wish I had a *chance*, that's all."

Do you now? And just what would you do with it? Let's check out the possibilities.

I would:

1. Jump right in with both feet and get even before the opportunity went away.
2. I'd ask God about it, and then hurry up and get even before He had a chance to answer.
3. I'd tell God I was going to get even and hope He would understand.
4. I'd tell God I *wanted* to get even, and then wait and see what He wanted me to do.
5. I wouldn't get even, but I'd feel pretty sore about it.
6. I wouldn't get even, and ask God to make me feel okay about it.

7. I wouldn't get even and I'd feel very cheerful about it—I think.
8. I might not get even the *first* time, but if the opportunity came again, I'm not so sure I could resist the temptation.
9. If the opportunity came again, I'd figure maybe God *wanted* me to get even.
10. I'd get even first and talk to God about it afterward.

David had that decision to make, and he came through with flying colors.[1] In fact he was so great that Saul crawled home feeling like a heel. And David came through the ordeal smelling like a rose. There was no doubt about it; it had been a great victory over temptation. And it should have kept Saul in his place for the rest of his life. Except for one thing.

Saul's memory.

It was very good when it came to holding grudges, but it was very poor when it came to remembering promises. So it wasn't very long before he began to think backwards and upside down again. Where was David? If he could only get his hands on David. Saul was like a firecracker looking for a place to explode. Now if you're looking for trouble, it's a sure thing you'll find it.

And Saul did.

Everything was going very well until some scouts from the town of Ziph called on Saul.[2]

"We have some valuable information as to David's whereabouts," they told Saul. And his nose twitched like a bloodhound that had just been given an old sock to smell.

"Where is he?" he asked.

"Well, he's returned to the wilderness—"

"Yes, yes?"

"And he's hiding on Hachilah (*Hatch*-i-lah) hill."

1. See chapter 2.
2. They were probably afraid of Saul. It was dangerous to "be on David's side."

30

Saul stared moodily ahead for a minute. And all the old jealousy and all the old hatred came back. His general, Abner, was standing across the room. He was looking at Saul and you could almost see the question marks coming out of his head. After David had spared his life, would Saul hunt him down again? Saul looked at Abner as if he could read his mind.

"Get ready," he said. "We'll hunt him down."

And off they went. Saul, and his general, Abner, and his bodyguard, and his scouts. And his elite[3] corps of three thousand troops.

David's spies, meanwhile, had not been sleeping. They kept him supplied with bulletins and late bulletins—he knew what was going on. So by the time Saul's army arrived and camped on the plain at the *edge* of the wilderness, David had edged his men farther *into* the wilderness and had sent out scouts to watch Saul's movements.

The game was about to begin.
David made the first move.
He took some of the men closest to him, and they started toward the place where Saul's army had set up camp. It was late at night. They crept through the night like shadows, without making a sound. At the edge, they parted some brush and looked down toward Saul's camp. It took only a moment to pick out where Saul was. He was sleeping inside a ring formed by his sleeping bodyguards. His spear had been mumbly-pegged into the dirt alongside him. It was a symbol of authority. It shone like silver in the moonlight. They waited a moment. No one moved. The air was still, except for the night bugs. "I'm going down," David whispered. "Any volunteers to go with me?"

"I'll go with you," a voice whispered back. It was Abishai (A-*bish*-a-i)—David's own nephew.

3. Really special, highly trained.

31

"All right," said David. "Let's go. The rest of you wait here."

Moments later they were within a stone's throw of that ring of soldiers. They crept closer.

Closer.

Nobody moved. Those soldiers were in a sleep so deep, there was only one answer for it.

The Lord had done it.

Abishai sucked in his breath. "The Lord has put your enemy in your power for sure this time." he whispered.

David said nothing.

"Let me go put that spear through him." Abishai went on. "Just let me at him. I'll pin him to the earth with it. He won't wake anybody up: he won't be able to. I won't need to strike a second time."

"No." David grabbed his arm. "Don't kill him. You *can't* kill him. He's God's chosen king. Don't lay a hand on him."

"But God has dumped him right in your lap."

"God will strike him down. And in His own way. And when He's good and ready."

"But what if He doesn't?"

"Then he will die of old age. But God forbid that I should kill the man He chose to be king."

Abishai sighed.

They were silent for a moment.

"I'll tell you what we *can* do," David said at last.

They took a step toward King Saul.

"We'll take his spear," David said. "And his jug of water. And that's all. And then we'll get out of here." David leaned over as he spoke. He grabbed the sword—and—

Pfffffft! Pulled it out of the ground. Then he picked up the jug of water and went back to Abishai, stepping carefully over the sleeping men. "Let's go," he said. "Let's get out of here."

And, silent as shadows, they disappeared into the darkness.

And, without a sound, they made their way toward the

hill again. When they were a safe distance away, David put his hand on Abishai's arm and signaled him to stop. They stood looking down at the camp for a minute. Everything was quiet, dead quiet. And then David's voice split the night.

"ABNER!" he shouted. "Wake up!" It sounded like the crack of doom.

Saul's general, Abner, struggled up on his elbow. "Who is it?" he shouted into the dark.

"Well, Abner, you're a fine fellow, aren't you?" David's voice came back. "Where in all of Israel is there a greater general than you?"

"Whaaa—?!?" started Abner.

"So why haven't you guarded your master the king when someone came to kill him?"

Abner sat bolt upright now, and looked over at Saul who was struggling to get up.

David laughed. "Well, this isn't good at all! Some general! You ought to die for your carelessness! If I were the king, I'd fire you! What kind of a warrior are you? Are you a man or a mouse? You're supposed to answer for the security of the king! He was in danger of getting killed and you lay there sleeping!"

The soldiers were all moving now—some of them were up on their elbows, some sitting up, some of them already getting to their feet. "I must have had a nightmare," Abner thought, "I'm glad I woke up."

But it wasn't a nightmare. The voice went on, booming through the night. "Where is the king's spear?"

Whattttt?!?

Abner looked over by Saul's head. The spear was gone!

"And the jug of water that was beside his head! Look and see!"

But Abner had already seen. The spear *and* the jug of water were gone.

Good grief.

It was David. It had to be David.

33

Saul thought the same thing. "Is that you, my son David?" he called out.

Oh, *no*. He was going to be *nice* again.

David's voice came back. And it was respectful. Right or wrong, Saul was the man God had put in authority over him. Saul was his king. "Yes, sire, it is," David said. And he called out again, but not in anger, "Why are you chasing me?" he cried. "What have I done? What is my crime? You've driven me away from my home, into a land where they worship heathen gods. Must I die on foreign soil? Why should you come out to hunt my life? You're hunting me down like a—like a *partridge* on the mountains!"

Saul was on his feet by now. He cupped his hands around his mouth. "I've done wrong!" he cried. "Come back home, my son. I'll no longer try to harm you."

There was no answer.

"You saved my life!"

No answer.

"I've been a fool, David, I've been a fool!"

No answer.

"And very wrong!"

Silence.

Then, "Here is your spear, sire," David said. "Let one of your young men come up here and get it. I don't need a reward from you. The Lord gives His own rewards for doing good and for being loyal. And I've been loyal to you, sire, I've been loyal!"

Abner had already signaled to one of the young men to go fetch the spear and the jug of water.

"Blessings on you, my son David!" Saul called out. The bushes crackled as the young man tore through them toward David. "You'll be a great conqueror!" Saul cried, but there was no answer, only the bushes crackling. It was a pretty speech and everyone knew it. And everyone knew that Saul didn't mean it.

After that a great quiet settled down over the night. The

34

soldiers mumbled and murmured, and finally went back to sleep again.

Before dawn, they were up and ready. By the time the sun was up, they were gone from the spot, already on their way back home.

David had had his chance to get even: his enemy had been dropped right into his lap. But he hadn't taken that chance. He hadn't lifted his hand against his king.

What Do You Think?

Getting a chance to get even is no big deal. It's when you decide you won't take that chance—that you *won't* try to get even—that you get to be ten feet tall. Getting even takes up a great deal of energy. And no matter how you might boast about it, down deep in your heart you feel that it wasn't so smart after all, that you just might have been a fool. Might be a lot smarter to spend that energy on something that is really going to do you some good. You might even *pray* for your enemies. One way or the other, the Lord will take care of them, you know.

He might even make some of them your friends!

How about that?

And how about memorizing:

". . . Never avenge yourselves. Leave that to God, for he has said that he will repay those who deserve it" (Rom. 12:19, *TLB*).

"When a man is trying to please God, God makes even his worst enemies to be at peace with him" (Prov. 16:7, *TLB*).

"Love your enemies! Pray for those who persecute you!" (Matt. 5:44, *TLB*).

Want to go over that list again—the one at the beginning of this chapter? What do you think now?

I WISH
MY PROBLEM WOULD END

CHAPTER 4/ 1 Samuel 27; 28:1-6; 29; 31; 2 Samuel 1

"I don't mind problems, but this one is ridiculous. It just goes on and on and *on*. There seems to be no end to it. I sometimes wonder if God is *ever* going to get it straightened out."

Well, David knew that his problem hadn't gone away yet. It was still on his back, like old man trouble. He kept thinking to himself, "No matter what Saul *says*—someday he's going to get me. The only way I can shake him off is to go back and live among the Philistines."

Which is exactly what he did.

And of all places—he went to Gath. And sought the protection of King Achish (*A*-kish).

But what a difference! The last time he'd been there, he'd been alone—a frightened refugee. And they had said, "Who needs him? Send him on his way!" And he had run for his life. But this time, he had six hundred men with him, *and* their families. And by now everyone knew that he was no longer in Saul's good graces.

37

So King Achish was delighted to have him on his side.

"Welcome," he said, "a royal welcome. Live in the royal city." And he rolled out the red carpet.

"If it's all right with you," said David, "we'd rather live in the suburbs." Which is exactly what they did.

In fact King Achish gave them a town all to themselves—a suburb by the name of Ziklag. So David and his family and his men and their families settled down and lived happily in the suburbs for over a year and a half.

During this time David was not just lolling in a hammock, either.

He and his men were secretly raiding idol-worshiping villages all around them. And David carefully neglected to tell King Achish. So what Achish didn't know was that David was quietly conquering and occupying towns—*for Israel.* He was just stashing them away for the future, you might say.

Now all of this sounds great—except for one thing.

David still had his problem with him.

He was still a refugee—exiled[1] from his own land. He still was not king as God had promised. And Saul was still out to skin him alive on sight.

Now you can see that all of this did not add up to h-a-p-p-y.

David trusted the Lord to work it out all right. But there must have been moments when he thought—*"When?!?"*

And then suddenly it all came to a head.

Out of the blue—"We're planning a major invasion into northern Israel," said King Achish.

"Oh?" said David.

"And I expect you and your army to be my bodyguard."

"Oh!" said David.

And David found himself and his six hundred men a part of an army such as he had never dreamed of. The chariots and horses of the Philistine army seemed to stretch out without

1. Kicked out of.

38

end. And the equipment! David had never seen anything like it!

And David's position? The rear guard. That's right. He brought up the rear, with King Achish.

The huge army started its march northward. The Philistine captains led their troops out first by battalions and companies. And David and his men marched at the rear with King Achish.

And then, suddenly—

The Philistine commanders stopped in their tracks; the wheels in their heads skidded to a screaming halt.

Wait a minute, *wait a minute!*

David and his men were marching at the *rear.*

Aaaauuuuugh.

"Hold it!" they shouted. "Halt!"

The order passed from battalion to battalion. "Halt!"

And the army came to a halt. And they bumped chariots and horses and heads and rears like a bunch of toppled dominoes.

"What are these *Israelites* doing here with us?" the captains demanded of King Achish.

"Why," said King Achish, "David is the runaway servant of King Saul of Israel. He's been with me for years. What's wrong with that?"

"It's *David*," they bellowed. "That's what's wrong with that. He's the one they sang about. 'Saul has slain his thousands, and David his ten thousands!' "

"Well?" said King Achish.

"Well," they cried, "when we get into the battle, he's going to be *behind* us and Saul will be in *front* of us. And we'll be in the middle. What's to prevent their squashing us between them in a giant pincer movement?[2] They could squash us between them like a bug!"

"All right, all *right*," said Achish. "I'll send him back."

2. Crush them from both sides—*crunch!*

39

He sent for David. "You're one of the finest men I've ever known," he began.

"Thank you," said David.

"But I have to send you home."

"What do you mean?" demanded David. "Why can't I help you fight your enemies?"

"Listen," said Achish. "As far as I'm concerned you're a perfect gentleman. But as far as my commanders are concerned D-a-v-i-d spells TROUBLE."

David just stood there staring.

"So get up early in the morning," Achish went on, "and leave as soon as it is light. And leave quietly. Please don't make a fuss. Don't upset my soldiers; they're upset enough already."

Well, there was nothing else to do. David gave his men their orders quietly. And the next morning they headed back into the Philistine country, back home. Or at least, it was the only home they knew.

David didn't know it, but his problem was about to be solved.

And Saul didn't know it, but doomsday was coming.

The Beginning of the End

The Philistine armies went on their way northward, up the plain near the coast. Then inland, through the valley of Jezreel, toward the Jordan River.

And then they saw Saul's army camped in the hills, to their right.

Camped in the *hills?*

Ah, no, the Philistines thought, those Israelites were not going to trick them into fighting in the hills. Not this time. In the hills, their chariots were no good. The tricky Israelites had always forced them to fight in the hills. They were in the valley and they intended to stay there.

The valley went deep into Israel.

And so did they—deeper, deeper—until they had split the country in half.

There they stopped and there they stayed. They had everything just the way they wanted it. The only way the Israelites could force them out would be to fight in the valley. And that meant they had to face the Philistine chariots.

What a horrible battle it was! The Israelites were slaughtered wholesale. The clashing of swords, the screams of horses, the whirrrr of arrows, the cries of men, and the crashing and buckling of chariots—all ran together in one big jangle of noise.

Saul strained his eyes to see through the dust of battle.

The din was so great it filled the skies. And no one heard Saul scream as the archers closed in on him and—
Whttttttt!

An arrow struck him, going deep, wounding him badly.

He clutched at himself and groaned to his armor bearer, "Kill me—please—kill me with your sword."

"I can't," cried his armor bearer, "I can't. I'm afraid to. I can't kill my king."

"But the Philistines will capture me. They'll torture me." he cried. "It's better to die!"

Saul's armor bearer stood there, pale with fright.

Then, with a great cry, Saul fell upon the point of his own sword, and it pierced him through.

The armor bearer waited.

His king was dead.

And then he too fell upon his sword beside Saul.

And there he died.

Saul no longer heard the cries of battle. Everything he had wanted all his life was gone. Everything he'd been so jealous of no longer mattered. Nothing mattered any more. His jealousy, his hatred, and all his bad wishes that had poisoned his mind and poisoned his whole life were swept aside in that battle. God had given him so much, and he had thrown

41

it all away. His kingdom was gone. And he was dead. And his sons were dead.

Three of them.

Only David was left—the shepherd boy who had been anointed king so many years before.

God Punished My Enemy—and Am I Ever Glad!

"I've been waiting for a long time for my enemy to get what was coming to him, the rascal."

You might as well know right off that this is *not* the right way to feel. "I'll Be Glad When You're Dead, You Rascal You" is all right in a funny song. But in real life it just doesn't work out.

David heard how the Israelite army had scattered in all directions like buckshot. And his heart squeezed down in pain.

And Jonathan—what of Jonathan?

Jonathan was killed too.

David's heart nearly burst with pain.

It was the end of his problem. But it was also the end of Saul, his king. And the end of the best friend he had ever had in his life—Jonathan.

He remembered when he was a shepherd boy in the hills, playing his flute and guiding his sheep. And how the prophet Samuel had anointed him the next king of Israel. He remembered playing his harp for Saul in the palace. He remembered when he'd first met Jonathan, and how they'd become friends closer than brothers.

And now Samuel was gone.[3] And Saul was gone. And Jonathan. Dear Jonathan.

David wrote a poem about it all, and set it to music. And sang it while he played his harp. And the music was sad and haunting.

He had never once been disrespectful to his king. He had

---

3. Samuel had died a couple of years before and all Israel had mourned him.

never once expected Jonathan to be disloyal to his own father. He had never once wished his enemies were dead. He had wished his *problem* would be solved. But he was willing to wait and let God solve it in His own way and in His own time.

No wonder God called David a man after His own heart.[4]

There was a new day dawning. A whole new life.

Never in all his wildest dreams could David ever imagine the glory that was ahead for him, and for Israel!

What About You?

God did seem to be taking His time about getting David's problem straightened out. What do you think? Do you think David might have been able to do the job faster? As long as God was being so slow, would it have been okay for David to take things into his own hands? Can you think of a problem you've had that looked as if it was never going to straighten out? Do you have a problem now that you feel isn't getting untangled quickly enough? Write it down. Can you think of anything you might be doing that is getting in God's way, keeping Him from handling it? Write it down. In what way can you leave this problem completely with God? Is it okay for you to fight for your rights? What do you think?

4. See Acts 13:22.

I WISH
THINGS WOULD GO SMOOTHLY—FOR ME

CHAPTER 5/ 2 Samuel 2:1–11; 5:1–25;
1 Chronicles 11:1–3; 12:23–40; Psalm 13; 1 Chronicles 14:1

"I wish things would go smoothly for *me*—like they do for the other guy. Some people just seem to lead some sort of a charmed life. Everything they do seems as smooth as cream."

Well, it does seem to be that way, sometimes. If you just take a slice out of a person's life, and it happens to be a *good* slice, it seems that way. But you're looking at just one slice—you're not looking at the whole thing.

Or if you could have had slides of David's life, and stopped on one slide, right at this point, it would look something like this:

Saul was dead.

There was nothing now to prevent David from being king.

"Shall I move back to Judah?" David asked the Lord.

And the Lord said, "Yes."

"Which city shall I go to?"

"Go to Hebron."

Hebron!

Why, this was where David's ancestor Abraham had lived, and built an altar to the Lord. Hebron lay in a fertile valley surrounded by hills—Hebron, loaded with some of the biggest grapes in all the world.

This was great! Everything was smooth as cream.

Except for one little problem.

Abner.

Abner was Saul's general—the one who was guarding Saul that unforgettable night when David sneaked down and took the king's spear and jug of water.[1] He was also the one who brought David to Saul after David killed the giant, Goliath.

Oh—*that* Abner.

Yes—*that* Abner. Saul's commander-in-chief.

That Abner had a one-track mind. He absolutely *hated* David. The idea of David's being crowned king was more than he could bear.

So before you could say, "Hand me my crown," Abner went to Mahanaim (May-ha-*nay*-im) on the other side of the Jordan, looked up Ish-bosheth (Ish-*bow*-sheth)—and crowned *him* king. And who was Ish-bosheth? He just happened to be Saul's very own son—the only remaining son who had not been killed.

Now there's trouble for you.

And to show David he wasn't fooling around, Abner continued Saul's war. He just picked it right up where Saul had left off. And he and his armies dedicated their lives to making David miserable. But they were like a flock of fruit flies buzzing in David's face. Just a nuisance. Nothing more. The Bible tells us "that was the beginning of a long war between the followers of Saul and David."[2]

How did it all come out?

Well, David became stronger and stronger.

And Ish-bosheth became weaker and weaker.

And to top it all off, Ish-bosheth was not exactly what you would call an expert in getting along with people. Within two years he'd made an enemy of Abner, so that Abner left him. And right after that, he was killed by two of his own military men, leaving the northern part of the kingdom (Israel) without a king.

1. He was probably there when David snitched the hem of Saul's robe, too.
2. Second Samuel 3:1.

46

The field was clear for David. The rest looked like smooth sailing. The elders of the rest of the tribes of Israel came to Judah to make David their king. So from here on out? Looked as smooth as cream.

Smooth Going!

What a celebration there was! It seemed as if all of Israel and Judah had turned out. They had certainly all sent their representatives. The leaders were there, and thousands of soldiers from every tribe of Israel. They all came pouring into Hebron.

The leaders went to David. "We're your relatives," they said. "As a matter of fact, even when Saul was king, you were the one who led our armies into battle and brought them safely back again. And the Lord your God has already told you, 'You shall be shepherd of My people Israel, you shall be their king.'"

David thought of the time, many, many years ago, when he was a mere shepherd boy—when the prophet Samuel had come into his father's house and anointed him the next king of Israel.

At last Samuel's prophecy had come true!

Happy Days Are Here Again!

Thousands of men from all the tribes in full battle array—all with a single purpose—

Making David the new king!

And the preparations that had been made for their arrival! People from nearby and faraway brought the food. On donkeys, on camels, on mules, on oxen, on their heads—

Huge supplies of flour and fig cakes and raisins and wine and oil and cattle and sheep—brought to the celebration.

For joy had spread throughout the land!

David the king had come home! Long live the king!

Smooth going! Smooth as cream!

Except for one little problem.

The tribes had to be brought together into one kingdom. And guess who had to do it? /
David.

—Or Are They?

Now this would take some doing.

First there was the matter of a capital. Hebron would no longer do. It was a wee bit too far down in Judah. They had to find some place that would be—that would be—

Jebus!

That was just the place. It was an Amorite-Hittite town that belonged neither to Judah nor Israel. About twenty miles north of Hebron. And almost in the middle of the whole country.

Just the place. Everything was going as smooth as cream.

Except for one little problem.

The Jebusites.[3] The Amorites and Hittites lived there. And they were not about to let it go.

The city itself was like a fortress. It was built on top of Mount Zion, and shut away by deep valleys on three sides. It was a *natural* for a fortress.

When the Amorites and Hittites heard that David was marching toward the city, they said, "*Who* David? David *who? Whom?*"

Indeed!

"Ho," they said, "you'll never get in here." And, "Ha," they said. "Why, we don't even have to send strong men out against you. Even our blind and lame could keep you out!" So they "ho'd" and they "ha'd" and they boasted. And while they were still boasting, David quietly gave orders to his troops. "Go up through the water tunnel into the city and destroy those lame and blind Jebusites."

And that's exactly what they did.

---

3. They were called "Jebusites" the way we are called "New Yorkers" or "Californians." But they were really Amorites and Hittites.

48

The Jebusites were *creamed.*

And he changed the name of the town. He called it the city of David. And later the name was changed to—JERUSALEM!

And then followed one of the most stupendous[4] building programs in the history of the kingdom! David built the city wider, longer, taller, than it had ever been built before!

Then King Hiram of Tyre offered to help. And the things that came pouring in! Cedar lumber! Carpenters! Masons! The material to build with and the experts to use them! And all to build a palace for David!

David became more and more famous and more and more powerful. For the Lord of the heavens was with him.

At last he was the king, at last he had arrived, at last he had everything. Things were as smooth as cream.

Except for one little problem.

What? Another Problem?

The Philistines were coming.

Yes, they really were. They had dominated Israel ever since Saul's defeat seven years earlier. And they had spread out all over the place, like locusts. When they knew David was king of Judah, they thought, "This is a nuisance." But when they found out that he had become king of all Israel, it was quite another matter. "This," they thought, "is ridiculous. David has *got* to *go!*" And they gathered their forces and started the march toward Jerusalem.

"Shall I go out and fight against them?" David asked the Lord. "Will you defeat them for me?"

And the Lord said, "Yes. Go ahead. I'll give them to you."

And that's just the way it turned out.

The Philistines spread out across the valley of Rephaim (*Ref*-ā-im).

And David went out there and pulverized them.

4. Whopping—super-big!

It was a whopping victory. But the Philistines were slow to learn. The dust had hardly settled, when they were back.

"They're back, Lord," said David, "and they're spread out all over the valley of Rephaim. What shall I do with them?"

And the Lord spoke to David. "Don't make a frontal attack." He said.

"No, Lord."

"Go behind them."

"Yes, Lord."

"And come out by the balsam trees."

"Yes, Lord."

"And wait. When you hear a sound in the tops of the trees—"

"What kind of a sound?"

"It will be a sound like marching feet."

"Marching *feet?*"

"You heard Me. When you hear the sound of marching feet—attack. The sound will be My signal that I have prepared a way for you. And that I will destroy them."

David did exactly as the Lord had instructed. And the result? The Philistines ran back to their own cities like whipped dogs with their tails between their legs. They realized by now that David was doing them a favor just to allow them to live in their own cities. And they had better *stay* in their own cities.

They could take a hint.

That was the last time they ever tried to invade Israel.

Problems! What're You Supposed to Do with 'Em?

The days of running were over. And the days of hiding were over. And the days of living in caves were over. And the days of living in heathen cities were over. And the grief was over. And the fear. And the pain. And the loneliness. David was home at last.

But not without problems.

David knew he was going to be king. God had told him so through the prophet Samuel. And he lived and he walked and he worked toward this goal. The problems he had were enough to make him sit right down by the roadside and quit. But he didn't quit. He kept going. He did not just keep going *between* problems. He kept going between problems and *during* problems. He trained his soldiers in guerrilla warfare. He drilled them and jumped them and marched them and climbed them until they were more agile[5] than mountain goats. But the most important thing to remember is that David's problems never drove him away *from* God—they drove him closer *to* God.

What About You?

Do you have problems? Do your problems seem to be pretty big right now? Do you resent[6] them? Do you really think that other Christians *don't* have problems? Well, do you honestly think it would be fair for you to be the only Christian in the world *without* problems?

Make a list of the problems that bug you most. Now alongside each problem, write down what you are doing about it. And in a third column, check yourself out. Is what you're doing, drawing you closer *to* God or farther *away* from Him?

Are you sitting by the wayside whining? Or are you training yourself so you'll be as agile as a mountain goat? Always remember this: No matter what your problems are or how hopeless they look to you, somewhere up ahead there's an *opportunity* coming. It may be just around the corner. If you spend your time whining, you won't be ready for it. Then you'll have *another* problem on your hands.

Watch it!

And remember—"Don't worry about anything; instead, pray about everything; tell God your needs and don't forget to thank him for his answers" (Phil. 4:6, *TLB*).

---

5. This means you can jump up, down and sideways with the greatest of ease.
6. Are you pretty sore about them?

51

I WISH
I COULD WORSHIP GOD—
MY WAY

CHAPTER 6/ 2 Samuel 6:1–19; 1 Chronicles 13; 15; 16

David was off to a roaring start. Israel was united at last—one great kingdom under one king. With a capital—Jerusalem—the city of David!

Now the city of David was great, as far as it went. But David wanted it to be the *holy* city; he wanted it to be the city of God.

So one more thing was needed.

The Ark.

The *Ark?!? What* Ark?

Why, the Ark of God, of course.

What? You don't know about the Ark of God?[1]

Why, the Ark was the beautiful golden box that Moses had been commanded to build way back when the Israelites were camped at the foot of Mount Sinai, after they'd escaped from Egypt. God gave Moses the directions for building the Tabernacle there, too, and the most holy piece of furniture in the Tabernacle was the Ark.

---

1. You can read all about it in the book, *Rules—Who Needs Them?*

53

What did the Ark look like?

Well, it was about the size of a huge steamer trunk. It was made of acacia wood and covered with gold, with gold cherubs on top, and a gold ring in each corner. When the Israelites traveled, the high priest and his sons covered the Ark with badgers' skins and a blue cloth. Then they put poles through the gold rings and carried it on their shoulders. It was uncovered only when it was safe inside a small room in the Tabernacle[2] and only the high priest was ever allowed to see it, and then only once a year.

What did it have inside?

Why, the Ten Commandments God had given to Moses. And a pot of manna the Israelites had eaten in the wilderness. And Aaron's rod that God had caused to bud way back in the wilderness.[3]

You see, the Ark stood for the presence of God.

It was very, very holy and sacred.

Now if they'd had newspapers back in those days, you could have followed the history of the Ark in headlines. And they might have gone something like this:

THE ARK GOES BEFORE THE ISRAELITES
    THROUGH THE WILDERNESS.
ARK CARRIED ACROSS THE RIVER JORDAN—ON
    DRY LAND!
ARK CARRIED AROUND CITY OF JERICHO—AND
    THE WALLS FALL DOWN!
JOSHUA PRAYS BEFORE THE ARK AFTER
    VICTORY AT MT. EBAL.
ARK KEPT IN THE TABERNACLE IN TOWN OF
    SHILOH.
ARK CAPTURED BY PHILISTINES!
ARK CAUSING SICKNESS AMONG THE
    PHILISTINES.

2. Called the holy of holies.
3. That's another story!

ARK RETURNED! RESTING AT THE HOUSE OF ABINADAB!

Yes sir. And that's where the Ark was when our story opens. In the house of Abinadab. In the town of Kirjath-jearim.

"I'll Serve You, Lord—"

The whole country was in a state of excitement. What a hubbub! Messengers were sent everywhere—over the mountains and through the valleys and across the rivers, into every tribe, into every nook and corner of the kingdom, to spread the news—

The Ark of God at last had a home to come to—Jerusalem!

And it was no small matter. It was indeed a big deal. David was asking for representatives from every tribe, every part of the country—all the VIP's were to be there. And they named the time.

At the appointed time, sure enough, the VIP's came streaming in from every direction—a huge convocation[4] gathered at the appointed place. They were organized, their provisions were packed, and at last the great day arrived and they were ready to go. To the house of Abinadab in the town of Kirjath-jearim.

Their object? To get the Ark of God and take it back to Jerusalem where it belonged. David had already constructed a tent to put it in.

"—But I'll Do It My Own Way"

At last the great moment arrived.

The first thing they did was to lift the Ark out of its place in Abinadab's house and put it on the brand new cart they'd brought along especially for that purpose. It was pulled by oxen.

What? No Levite priests? No poles through golden rings?

4. A BIG crowd like "standing room only."

And what? On a *cart?!?* Why, the heathen nations carried their *idols* on carts! Such a business!

Trouble, no?

Trouble, *yes*. Wait and see.

Well they lifted the Ark—hup—and put it on the brand new cart—ooops—and they were ready to go. Abinadab's sons—two chaps by the names of Uzza (*Uh*-zah) and Ahio (A-*high*-o)—took charge of driving the oxen.

The orders were given, and the procession got started. The oxen started forward and the cart jerked and then began to rumble along behind, the Ark swinging and swaying precariously.[5]

They were off to a start, but it was a bad one.

Off they went, Ahio walking in front, followed by David and the VIP's of Israel.

And talk about joy!

It was one of the greatest days of their lives! It was a noisy parade, but the noise was the noise of joy. They were waving branches of juniper trees and playing every sort of musical instrument before the Lord—lyres, harps, tambourines, castanets, cymbals—you name it, they had it. And the sound! It was like turning up the volume on a stereo so a whole city block could hear it!

Now this was no easy accomplishment, for Kirjath-jearim was built high in the hills and the trip was all *down*hill. But on their way they went, the oxen slipping and struggling to keep their footing, and the cart swaying and tipping first to one side and then the other as the wheels rumbled up and down over rocks and sank in potholes.

The procession went on, and David and his men sang out—and the sound of their voices and their instruments rang out, around, sideways, and up, till it reached the sky.

When suddenly—

5. Pretty shaky.

"Whoa—WHOA—Hold it—HOLD IT!!!"

What was this?

"Oooops—My Way Isn't Working"

David skidded to a stop, digging his heels into the ground.

More shouting. "Hold it! Whoa! Hold iiiiiittttt!"

Men stopped so fast that those behind them rammed into them, climbed up their backs and bumped their heads. One by one the instruments stopped playing. And the singing stopped and the oxen stopped and the cart stopped and everything and everyone stopped, just stopped.

Then David got his footing, whirled around and sprinted back like a runner out to win the hundred-yard dash. And everyone sprang into action again.

There were hurried questions and heavy breathing as men ran back—like running back to the scene of an accident.

"What happened?"

"I don't know."

"What were they shouting about?"

"Something happened—something bad."

"Yeah—it sounds bad."

"Let me through."

David ran ahead of everyone else. His heart sank. Had someone fallen? Had they run into an ambush? Were they being attacked by snipers?

Or had something happened to the Ark?

Oh, no—not *that*, he thought. And he quickened his pace.[6]

He got back to where the cart was. His heart sank. He stopped short. That's where the crowd was gathered, around the cart.

No—*no.*

The men began to make way to let him through. Those in the back were on tiptoe, ogling, trying to see over the heads of those in front.

6. He ran like mad, and you'd better believe it.

57

"What happened to him? Did he get hit?"

"He fell?"

"I don't know. Let King David through. Out of the way. Let him through. Hey! Let him through!"

Those in the front of the crowd were staring at something—someone, on the ground.

"He touched the Ark. He reached out and touched it."

"The oxen stumbled. And the cart began to tip."

"He reached out to steady it."

"He touched it with his hand."

David got to the front at last. And stopped.

It was Uzza. He was sprawled on the ground beside the cart. And he was very, very dead.

David stared at him in unbelief.

"What happened?" he asked, although he already knew.

They told him again. "The cart tipped. He reached out to steady it. He—touched it. He touched the Ark of God."

"I Did It All Wrong"

Now some things are called mishaps and some things are called problems and some things are just plain pesky, and you manage to put up with them somehow and get on with the job.

If it had just rained on David's parade, they could have put their instruments under tarps and bedded down for the night and somehow carried on. Or even if they'd been caught in ambush and there were enemy snipers about, they could have called upon God. They'd been in scrapes like *that* before.

But this was none of those things. This was deadly serious. This was tragic.

Now when you get that much adrenalin[7] in your blood, then you've got to react somehow.

---

7. Adrenalin is a little juice the adrenal gland pours into your bloodstream when you are frightened, or angry, to give you extra strength. It's sort of like "fuel injection" on a car.

And David reacted.

Anger.

He felt it starting way down inside him, and then boiling up. Anger.

All he was trying to do was to bring the Ark home to Jerusalem. Why had God done this terrible thing? All this planning, all this organization, all this work, for nothing. From his toes, he felt it boiling up. Anger.

And then fear.

He slumped suddenly as if somebody had stuck a pin in him and let all his air out.

All the plans and all the work and all the organization—had been his own. He had put the holy Ark of God on a *cart*. With all his good intentions he was *fooling around* with the holy Ark of God!

Now the fear was greater than the anger.

"How can I ever bring the Ark home?" he cried.

There was silence. Nobody answered. Everybody had been struck absolutely dumb with shock. David lifted his head, staring into space, saying nothing for a moment.

Then finally, "Make a stretcher for Uzza," he said quietly. "And then we'll march on."

"To Jerusalem?" they asked.

"No," said David. "To the house of Obed-edom (O-bed-*eee*-dom). We'll leave it there."

Which is exactly what they did.

"I've Bungled It for Good"

In Jerusalem the people waited for the return of David and his men—and the Ark of God. They knew when they saw the procession coming in the distance that something was wrong. There was no music. There was no joy. The procession came silently, silently, toward the city—marched in the gate—

There were no shouts from the people in the city either.

59

There were only muttered questions and muttered answers—and weeping over Uzza—

The word spread throughout the city, up one street and down another—from one home to another. The Ark of God had been left back at the home of the Levite priest, Obededom. When would it come into Jerusalem? No one knew. King David wasn't saying. The people turned in early and closed their shutters. Every house was a house of mourning.

King David went to his palace, silent and shaken. Far into the night, after everyone else in the palace was asleep, he sat alone in the dark. And thought over what he had done.

Everything he'd ever been taught came back to him. The Ark was the most holy thing that represented God to the people of Israel.

It was to be carried *only* by Levite priests on poles.

It was *never* to be touched.

It was *not* to be taken lightly.

It was the *holiest* of all holy things.

And he had bustled about, making his own plans, toting it on a cart as if it were a piece of merchandise. His *intentions* were good—but he had done it his own way. For the first time in his life he had taken God lightly.

He put his head in his hands and sat there alone and silent.

For the first time in his life, he was afraid of God.

"Can I Make Another Try?"

It took a while for David to unscramble all the things in his mind. The days went into weeks. Then months. He went about the business of being king, a little on the quiet side. He knew God had forgiven him, but there was one thing more he knew for sure. If ever he brought that Ark into Jerusalem, he wanted to do the job right—if ever he could see his way clear.

And then one day the whole sorry business cleared up like a bright morning after a storm. It was a report he received—a routine report. But it meant everything in the world to him.

The Ark was safe and doing well at the home of Obed-edom. But that wasn't all. God was blessing Obed-edom as he'd never been blessed before. And that wasn't all. God was blessing his whole household. And his family. And his servants. And everything he touched.

Eureka!

This was it!

The storm was over, the morning had come. All the signals said go, go, go.

"All Right, Lord, I'll Do It Your Way"

Jerusalem was abuzz with excitement. They'd been waiting for days for the Ark to arrive. David had gone out four days before with his men to get it. The people on the watchtowers and on the city walls could see them coming like specks in the distance, long before they heard the music.

It was the crash of the cymbals they heard first. And then the tambourines. Then the harps and lyres. And the castanets.

And the singing!

And the dancing!

David was heading the whole procession and he was dancing and leaping into the air for sheer joy. And the sound of music was enough to make their eardrums wobble!

As the procession entered the city of David, the choirs began to sing.

Yes, choirs! There was more than one choir—there were many choirs, answering each other.

"Lift up your heads, O ye gates; . . . and the King of glory shall come in—

"Who is this king of glory?

"The Lord God almighty—the Lord mighty in battle—!"[8]

And the Ark was coming, the Ark was coming! Covered with a veil. And the badgers' skins. And the blue cloth. With

8. From Psalm 24:7,8.

the poles put through the golden rings. And carried on the shoulders of the Levite priests.

The glory of God was coming into the city of Jerusalem!

The singers in the choirs nearly burst their throats! And as the Ark went by, the people shouted for joy. And some of them wept. And the Ark was carried up the street, into the solemn place that David had prepared for it—the tent, like the old Tabernacle in the wilderness.

It was carried carefully inside. And the very tent became the holy of holies because it was there.

And the people feasted and sang and gave thanks to God. What a day!

"You Put It All Together, Lord"

When the great celebration was over, David sent them home, each with a gift—a loaf of bread, some wine, and a cake of raisins. And when everyone had gone and it was all over, David returned to bless his family.

All the pieces fell into place. The parents were the rulers over the children. The government and the courts were the rulers over the parents. And David was the king over all Jerusalem, and all of Israel.

But God was the ruler over *all*.

What About You?

"Phew! Boy! Did *he* ever blow it!"

"I never would have done that!"

Well, then, have you ever done *this?* Fooled around in Sunday School? Like untying the shoes of the guy next to you? Or wrestling while your student book and your Bible slide to the floor, under the seat of the girl next to you? Did you smirk and giggle when you couldn't find it? And everyone knew where it went but you? And the teacher asked you to look up something?

The Bible is the holy Word of God.

Or have you ever run through the aisles of Sunday School

or down the aisles of church yelling things that are okay on the school playground *but*—the church is the holy house of God.

What's this? Doesn't God want you to have any fun? You bet your sweet life He does. Jesus' middle name is JOY. And His name is LOVE. And His name is VICTORY. Really knowing Jesus is like shouting and singing and soaring into the very air. Everything God has to give you is right off the top, first class, highest quality, the very best.

You just have to be careful how you handle it, that's all.

David was the *king*. But God was his boss.

It's the same way with you.

Just remember, when you worship Him—He's the boss. He writes the script. You don't.

Get it?

Remember, "This plan of mine is not what you would work out, neither are my thoughts the same as yours! For just as the heavens are higher than the earth, so are my ways higher than yours, and my thoughts than yours" (Isa. 55:8,9, *TLB*).

I WISH
OTHER PEOPLE WOULD
KEEP THEIR PROMISES

CHAPTER 7/ 2 Samuel 9; 1:4; 1 Chronicles 10:1–8

"When I make some promises I really mean to keep them. Promises like 'If I get to be class president, I'll remember you, my friend, for campaigning for my votes.' Or, 'If I ever get that scholarship for camp, I'll put in a good word for you.' Or, 'When I get that money my father promised me, I'll pay you back.'

"But then when the time comes, I forget it. Or I just hope the *other* guy will forget it.

"Of course I always wish that *other* people would keep *their* promises."

Of course.

This is a story of a man whose very life depended on a promise—and whether or not the *other* guy would keep it.

_____

The house of the prince was strangely quiet. It wasn't just *quiet* quiet. It was *spooky* quiet.

There was a spirit of fear in the air.

Mephibosheth (Mee-*fib*-o-sheth) tried to understand what was going on. It wasn't easy. He was only five years old.

There was a war on—that much he knew. Israel was slugging it out with the Philistines. But Israel had battled with the Philistines before during his life. Never before, though, had there been this—this—*feeling*. His heart seemed squeezed down inside him and he felt like crying. But he was the son of a prince, and prince's sons aren't supposed to cry.[1] Whatever happened, he knew one thing. He had to live up to his name. And his name (Mephibosheth?!?) was enough to make any little guy round shouldered just carrying it around, without being a prince's son to boot. On this particular day he felt the burden was almost too much to bear.

He made a pretense of playing with his toys, but his eyes were on swivels, studying the face of his nurse. What was written on her face? Was she sick? Was she sad?

No. She was just plain scared. There was no sense fooling himself.

Mephibosheth left off playing and wandered down the hall.

People were sneaking about as if something dreadful was about to happen. Servants, soldiers, guards—everyone was on tiptoe, as if waiting for something. Before he had time to ask one question, nurse was right behind him. And before you could say, "What's cooking," she had whisked him off to the nursery again.

"WHAT'S GOING ON?" he asked.

'Shhhhh.'

"What's going on?" he whispered. "Is my father all right? Is my grandfather all right? What's going on?"

"Shh!" she said again. It was a short "Shh" this time, but she meant it. And then she saw his frightened face. She sat down on the broad window seat and drew him to her. "The brave soldiers are fighting a battle with the Philistines," she

1. Not so you could notice it, anyhow.

said. "And you know that your father and your grandfather are the bravest soldiers of all."

"Yes, I know."

"You must be brave too."

"Yes, ma'am, I know." But fear clutched him again inside, tightening. He must be brave too, she'd said. That meant only one thing. The battle was going badly.

Why? he wondered. His grandfather Saul was the *king*. And he was a king who did not go about losing battles. And his father Jonathan was the bravest man in the whole world. Why, he had attacked the Philistines singlehanded once, with only his armor bearer. They had scrambled down one cliff, across the pass, and up the other cliff and lighted into the Philistines—and *belted* them! And God had sent along an earthquake to finish the job![2] Why, his father wasn't afraid of anybody.

Mephibosheth began to think aloud. "My father is the bravest man in the world," he began. "Why, he even—"

But she wasn't listening. A soldier had stuck his head in the doorway, and she had risen so hurriedly she had almost dumped Mephibosheth on the floor.

"King Saul is dead." The soldier had said it in a low voice, but Mephibosheth had heard it. His nurse turned the color of the parchment he wrote his lessons on. Her hand went to her throat. "And Prince Jonathan?" she asked. The soldier just shook his head. The nurse and the soldier were speaking hurriedly now, their words tumbling out. Fast, fast, as if there were no time to lose, not even a second.

"I have some guards ready. They're waiting to take you. Hurry downstairs."

"Where?" she said, as she hurried about the nursery, gathering up things. A blanket for Mephibosheth. A shawl for herself. A toy. A *toy?* No one who was thinking would pick up a toy at a time like this. Nurse's thinker had gone on

2. You can read about this in *Rules—Who Needs Them?*

automatic pilot. Mephibosheth was glued to the spot with fear. His grandfather Saul dead! And his father, his father!

"FATHER!!!" he screamed.

His scream was smothered in her shoulder as she swooped him up in her arms and began to run down the hall.

"Hurry!" the soldier said, running ahead. She didn't answer. She was sobbing now, running after him.

What happened next, happened too quickly for Mephibosheth to even feel fear. He felt her stumble. She loosened her hold on him. He fell to the floor, smashing into it. And she fell too, sprawling. She scrambled to her feet, gathered him up again and ran down the hall, sobbing.

And then he felt the pain. He'd been hurt, terribly hurt. His feet felt as if they'd been broken. He had only fallen from his nurse's arms. But he felt as if he'd been dropped from a roof. He began to cry with fear and rage and pain. She didn't shush him. They were outside now, and the guards were hoisting him and his nurse up on a donkey. Without a word, they all scurried off, down the path, through the bushes, toward the house of Machir in the town of Lo-debar.

I'm in Trouble—Except for a Promise

It was almost evening. The servants began to light the candles. Everyone spoke in whispers. And the people of the house gathered around as nurse bathed Mephibosheth's feet. Always he would remember it. When they had lifted him off the donkey and set him on his feet, he had cried out in pain. His feet! He couldn't stand on his feet!

He'd stopped crying hours before. He lay there now whimpering like a hurt puppy. And everyone still talked in whispers. Over and over again they talked about it. King Saul was dead. Prince Jonathan was dead. And poor little Mephibosheth was alone. He would be brought up with a houseful of servants and teachers, as a prince's son should.

A prince's son?

His grandfather Saul had been the king. And he was dead.

And his father had been the prince. And *he* was dead.

And David would be the new king!

Where did that leave Mephibosheth? Well, he was too young to know it, but that left him out in the cold. His title as a prince had about as much zap in it as yesterday's soggy cereal. No power in it at all. Not a snap, not a crackle, not a pop. He was as good as dead.

Wait a minute. He *was* as good as dead. When a *new* king came into power, one of the first things he did was kill all the members of the *old* king's family, so none of them could step forth and claim the throne!

That's why everyone was looking at him so strangely. And that's why they were speaking in whispers. And that's why every time his nurse looked at him, her eyes filled with tears. Why, Mephibosheth's life hung on one thing—

A promise!

Yes, David had made Jonathan a very important promise.[3] And Mephibosheth's very life depended on whether or not he would keep it.

Phew!

If ever a guy could hope the *other* guy would keep his promise, that little guy would be Mephibosheth.

And if ever a group of people kept tabs on what was going on in the country, it was the people responsible for bringing up Mephibosheth there in the house of Machir.

If there had been newspapers in Israel at that time, the headlines might have gone something like this:

DAVID CROWNED KING OF JUDAH.

DAVID NOW KING OF ALL ISRAEL!

DAVID ESTABLISHES JERUSALEM AS CAPITAL OF ISRAEL.

DAVID BUILDS PALACE IN JERUSALEM.

DAVID BRINGS ARK OF GOD INTO JERUSALEM!

---

3. He had promised to look after Jonathan's children if Jonathan died. You can read all about it in the book, *Rules—Who Needs Them?*

Yes, they decided, the only smart thing to do was to keep Mephibosheth hidden. And when he grew up, he decided the same thing. The only smart thing to do was to keep out of the way. David seemed like a man who would keep his promise—but you couldn't be sure. And by the time you found out he might *not*—it would be too late.

Mephibosheth was more or less happy. But there were two dark clouds. One, he was never able to go back to his father and grandfather's home. And two—his feet had never healed properly. He was a cripple.

There was one bright spot in all this. King David did not know that he existed.

So as the years went by, the fear of being discovered grew smaller and smaller and smaller—

Until finally it wasn't there at all.

And that was when the bad news came.

It descended upon him like a thunderbolt. And it sent him, and his old nurse, and all the folks in Machir's house—into a tailspin.

But What About the Guy Who Made the Promise?

But—

Little did he know—

King David sat in one of the huge rooms in his palace in Jerusalem. He was with his advisers, and they were going over the business of the day. So many things had been accomplished. They had subdued the Philistines, established a capital city, built a beautiful palace, brought home the Ark of God—

Now they had a little breathing spell where they could pick up the loose ends and do all the little odd jobs that had been neglected. It was time to sort of tidy up. The meeting had gone on all morning and they had checked a long list of things to be done.

"I think that's about all, sire," said David's chief adviser. And he turned to leave the room.

70

"Wait a minute," said David. "Before you go."

"Yes, sire?"

"There is something else. Something I've thought of many times. Is Jonathan's family all gone? Is there anyone left? Did he have any children? Did he have any sons?"

Ah! This was it. If any former king had any sons, their heads would be lopped off before you could say, "Long live *what* king?"

"I don't know, sire," was the reply. "But there is a man around who was one of Saul's chief servants. Fellow by the name of Ziba."

Well, Ziba was sent for in great haste. And King David got right to the point. "I want to know about Jonathan's family," he said. "Are there any left?"

"There is one living, sire," said Ziba. "Jonathan's son."

"Oh?"

"Yes. His name is Mephibosheth. He's a young man now."

"Where is he?"

"He's at the home of Machir. In Lo-debar. But he can do you no harm, sire. He is crippled."

David leaned forward. "How did it happen? In battle?"

"No, no, sire. It happened when he was a little boy. Only five years old. It happened the very day Saul and Jonathan died. His nurse was trying to escape with him. She was carrying him. She fell. And dropped him."

"Well?"

"His feet were badly hurt. He has never been able to walk properly."

There was silence as David thought about everything he had meant to Jonathan. And everything Jonathan had meant to him. What friends they had been! Never had two boys been firmer friends. Never had two young men been so close—closer than many brothers ever could be. "Send for him," David said at last. "And bring him to the palace. I want to see him."

Will He Keep It?

When the messenger arrived at Machir's home, it seemed as if the very bottom had dropped out of Mephibosheth's life. "King David has sent for you," the message said. "He wants you to come to the palace in Jerusalem."

King David!?

Mephibosheth knew he would have to go. This was the end of everything.

—This *was* the end of everything—but not the way Mephibosheth thought!

He Kept It, He Kept It!

When Mephibosheth and his servants went through the gates of Jerusalem, he felt as if he was going to his doom. When he entered the palace, he didn't see the beauty of it. When he was brought into the presence of the king, he was one big bundle of fear. His very life hung on the promise of this great man. And now it looked as if his life was finished. King David would never keep that promise now. It would be too dangerous for him to do so; there was too much at stake. Mephibosheth bowed to the ground before the great king.

This was it!

"Lift your head," said David. "Look at me."

Mephibosheth looked up at the strong face of the great king. The ruddy skin was darkened to bronze by now. It was a bit craggy[4] but there were lines of strength in it—and lines of suffering too. And tenderness.

"You are Mephibosheth," David said.

"Yes, sire."

"Jonathan's son."

"Yes, sire."

"I sent for you," said David. "I made your father a promise."

4. Sort of busted up in little creases.

72

Mephibosheth couldn't answer. He was holding his breath.

"I promised your father, that if anything ever happened to him—I would take care of his children. He promised the same thing—that if anything ever happened to me, he would take care of mine. Well, something did happen to him. And I want to keep my promise."

What? Wanted to keep his promise? Wow!

Mephibosheth was absolutely overcome with relief. He bowed himself to the ground again. "Who am I," he said, "that you should look upon such a dead dog as I am."

"Get up," the king said softly. Mephibosheth struggled to his feet with great difficulty and stood, leaning upon a servant.

And the next thing he knew, Ziba was coming into the room. Why, Ziba was his grandfather's chief steward who ran his household!

"Ziba," David was saying, "I have given Mephibosheth all that belonged to King Saul. All that belonged to his grandfather now belongs to him."

This was incredible![5] Mephibosheth pinched himself secretly. He *must* be dreaming. Or the king must be out of his mind to let Saul's grandson live. It would be dangerous. There were still people in the kingdom who favored Saul and would like to see someone in Saul's family back in power. Why, Mephibosheth could gather a following and still try to take the throne away from David—and he would now have the wealth to try it! David had lost his marbles!

"Ziba," the king was saying, "you'll farm the land for him, you and your sons and your servants. But Mephibosheth will live here in the palace with me. He will be like one of my own sons."

Good grief! Now Mephibosheth had not only the wealth but the position! He'd be right in the palace! The king *had* lost his marbles.

---

5. Almost impossible to believe, like, "You've got to be kidding!"

David had gone against all tradition.[6] Instead of killing the son of the former king, he had saved him, restored his wealth and position, and was inviting him to live right in the palace!

Nutty, yes?

Nutty, no.

Things like that simply didn't happen. But then friendships like the one between David and Jonathan didn't happen very often either.

Already the servants were scurrying about to carry out David's orders. This thing was for real. Mephibosheth finally had to believe it. He looked at David. And his look seemed to say, "Aren't you afraid of what I might do?"

And David looked back. And his look seemed to say, "I'll take that chance. A promise is a promise."

Phew!

The days of hiding and dreading what would happen were over at last. All his life—since he was a little boy of five—Mephibosheth had lived with a shadow hanging over him. At any time the king might hear of his whereabouts, and decide to do what new kings always did—

Kill him.

So you might say he'd been living his life under a sentence of death—a marked man. And what he'd never known was that his life had hung upon one thing—

A promise.

You wish other people would keep their promises? You can bet your life—that if Mephibosheth had known what was at stake, he'd have wished the same thing!

For the promise the "other person" had made concerning him was a promise that meant his very life!

What About You?

Want to go back and read the first section of this chapter

6. The way people always did it.

74

again? What do you think now? Is it important for other people to keep their promises? Well, then, is it important for *you* to keep *yours?*

Will you promise yourself that you'll memorize this verse? It's a promise meant for you—from God.

"And he himself has promised us this: eternal life" (1 John 2:25, *TLB*).

But you must do *your* part.

"And this is what God says we must do: Believe on the name of his Son Jesus Christ" (1 John 3:23, *TLB*).

Don't fudge. Did you keep your promise?

I WISH
I WERE A BIG SHOT

CHAPTER 8/ 2 Samuel 14:25,26; 15—19:15; 1 Kings 1:6

"I always wanted to be a big shot—you know, somebody really important. Sometimes I daydream about it. And sometimes I lie awake and think about it. I imagine all sorts of things, like I conquered everything and I've become the leader and everybody has to kowtow to me, or else. Of course, I know it isn't easy to be a big shot. And in my daydreams I always have to 'mow a few people down.' You know—people get in your way.

"That's the trouble, though. In my *real* life—even when I'm not daydreaming, I'd like to be a big shot. But then, people get in my way there too.

"I don't like to come right out and say it, but there are times when even my parents get in my way. I wish sometimes that they'd let me do as I please. Maybe my whole life would turn out differently."

Well, don't feel too guilty about these thoughts; they're pretty normal. If you've wished any of these things, you're at the end of a long, long line. We've all wished them at some time or another, if only in our daydreams. Of course, along with the wish that you could be a big shot is the wish that everybody who is bugging you would get out of your way. And even though you don't like to admit it or talk about it, you have a sneaking feeling that maybe you *could* be a big shot, if only they'd stop holding you back.

Don't feel guilty. Remember the old Chinese proverb—"You can't keep the birds from flying over your head, but you can keep them from building a nest in your hair."

And speaking of hair, the lad in this chapter had a lot of it. His name was Absalom, and his hair was thick and absolutely beautiful. Of course, lots of people have hair that is thick and beautiful, but the thing that set him apart was that he had so *much* of it. He cut it once a year, and then only because it was too much of a load to carry around. The wind resistance was terrific. In the hundred-yard dash, he would have needed a tail wind to get him around the track. He cut it and then he *weighed* it. And it weighed two hundred shekels by the king's weight.[1]

Now all this hair didn't do him any good. It wasn't a sign of strength as it had been in Samson, for instance. But it sure did make him easy to single out in a crowd. At forty paces it was easy to tell who he was. You can see that Absalom had more things going for him than a centipede has legs. He was good-looking, tall, handsome, smart—and he had the kind of personality that drew other people to him like a light draws moths. Wherever he was, people gathered around to be near him. He could have won a popularity contest with a bag over his head. Everything he said was clever. And everything he did was a little bit better than anyone else could do it. And to top it all off—he was the king's son! And

1. Three pounds!

not just *any* king's son. He was the son of the most popular king Israel had ever known.

His father was King David.

So Absalom didn't have to dream about being a big shot. He already *was*. And he didn't have to try harder—he was already number one.

Now it seems incredible[2] that somebody who had all that going for him would have to go and spoil it all.

But this is exactly what Absalom started out to do.

He became a smart aleck.

Now a smart aleck is going to cause trouble wherever he is. But when he does his smart-alecking around a place where someone is trying to run a government[3] he can cause more trouble than anywhere else.

"I Can Be More Important Than He Is"

Well, you can see right off that when you start thinking like a smart aleck, you're headed for trouble. "What? What do you mean? Isn't it okay to try to be the best in your field?" Of course it is. It's okay to want to try to be the best you can in whatever it is you're doing. But there's a difference between wanting to be *good* at something and wanting to be the *most important* person in the place, wherever it is. This, alas, is what Absalom was up to. If he'd wanted to be more important than his friends it would have been bad enough. But he wanted to be more important than—of all people—his own father!

King David!

There was no way this could be done except by scheming and mischief—and just plain old hanky-panky.

Hanky

Absalom started out with his dirty plot in grand style. He

2. Hard to believe. Remember?
3. Or a church. Or a school, for that matter.

bought a magnificent chariot. And chariot horses. And as if that weren't enough, he hired fifty footmen to run ahead of him.[4] You can see that underneath Absalom's beautiful hair was a mean little head. You'd have to get up pretty early in the morning to carry out all the mean little schemes *in* that mean little head. Which is exactly what Absalom did.

He got up early every morning, pranced out to the gates of the city—and stopped. It was the end of his journey.

The spot by the gates of the city was called the "broad place" and it's where all the people gathered, business was carried on, decisions were made, and all the gossip was swapped. If you wanted to find out anything about anything, you went to the broad place. And mingled with the crowds. And listened.

Well, Absalom was there, early every morning. He got out of his chariot and greeted the people, including all newcomers who came in the gate.

"Where're you from?" he'd ask.

"Oh, from such-and-such a tribe," they'd say.

"I *see!*" he'd say, pretending to be very interested. "And what is your problem?"

Well, they'd tell him their problem and he'd listen and cluck and strut. "I can see that you're right in this matter," he'd say. "It is *most* unfortunate that the king doesn't have anybody to assist him in hearing these cases."

Yes, most unfortunate indeed. And what was wrong with the king? And why didn't he have someone to assist him in such matters? Absalom didn't come out and *say* this. But he made everybody *think* it. "Ah," he would sigh. "I wish I were the judge. Then anyone with any problem at all could come to me, and *I* would straighten everything all out. (Sigh) I wish every man would come to me."

Ah, yes indeed. Absalom was as clever a politician as ever lived. He would have been kissing babies and having his

4. What a sneaky way to spend your allowance!

picture taken. Except that kissing babies hadn't been thought of yet. And cameras hadn't been invented. And when anyone bowed to him, Absalom wouldn't hear of it. He shook the chap's hand instead. And clapped him on the shoulder. And treated him as an equal. You might say he was a good interceptor. Before the passes ever reached the king, Absalom intercepted them and made for his own goal line.

And his own goal?

Why, *he* wanted to be king—of course!

How could anyone do this to his own dad? Well, it *is* hard to believe. But it's exactly what Absalom wanted to do. The Bible tells us that he kept up this business until he had turned the loyalties of many people away from his father, King David—to himself.

A great many people.

Too many people.

There was trouble ahead.

Panky

"Father," said Absalom, "I have a request to make of you."

"Yes, my son," said David. "Ask whatever you will. Your wish will be granted."

"I want to go to Hebron," said Absalom innocently. "I want to make a sacrifice to the Lord—and worship Him."

Nothing wrong with that. Nothing suspicious. Hebron was Absalom's hometown.

"Yes, my son," said David. "Go to Hebron in peace; go with my blessing."

Absalom bowed his way out of his father's presence. And got ready. He invited two hundred friends to go with him; they started packing at once. The friends just thought they were going on a pleasant trip to Hebron; they didn't know they were part of the mischief.

But mischief it was—black, black mischief.

Absalom was no sooner in Hebron, than he sent secret messengers to every part of Israel. And the message? You're not going to believe it! "As soon as you hear the trumpets," the message read, "you will know that Absalom has been crowned king in Hebron."

Outrageous? Outrageous! Why, that rascal Absalom had a whole network of secret supporters for the messengers to contact. He hadn't just been making mischief in the city gates; he'd been making mischief over the country! Yes—and even the very palace! Yes—some of his supporters were men closest to the king himself!

For the very next thing he did was to send for Ahithophel (A-*hith*-o-fell). And who in the world was Ahithophel? Why, he was one of David's advisers who lived in Giloh.

AhHAH. This plot *was* getting thick!

—And Pow!

It was at this point that all of Absalom's hanky-panky blew up in David's face. One minute he was sitting on his throne, ruling his kingdom and trusting his dear son Absalom and thinking all was well with the world. And the next minute a messenger came. And said something that shattered his world into little bits.

WOOOSH! Absalom had *not* gone to Hebron to sacrifice to the Lord.

WHAM! He had gone there to set up a rebellion against his father. The idea was to make himself king.

ZAP! He already had a network of spies and willing con-spirators[5] throughout the whole nation.

SOCK! He was about to declare himself king. And he was already on his way—marching against Jerusalem!

AUUUGH! Rebellion! War. And the enemy attacking was David's own son Absalom!

David's world was shattered and came completely apart and the splinters flew in all directions.

5. Partners in his hanky-panky.

It was a staggering blow, worse than anything he'd ever got from King Saul.

Absalom!

Come Out of Your Corner Fighting

It would seem that David was licked, that he did not have a chance. Nearly all of Israel was with Absalom. But David was no ordinary person. He was a champion. And the difference between an ordinary person and a champion is that the champ *keeps on fighting after he's been licked.*

David's heart was absolutely smashed over what his son Absalom had done to him. But this was no time to cry. So David put his heart on automatic pilot. And started using his head.

"We have to get out of Jerusalem," he said. "If we fight here, the city will be destroyed. We can organize better—and fight better, outside."

He was thinking, he was thinking.

No one questioned his decision. "We are with you," his officials replied. "Do as you think best."

This was no time for anger: this was no time for fear. This was time for grim determination.[6]

David gave his orders quietly, and kept his head. So those who were following him took his orders and kept their heads too.

The evacuation of the great city was a sad one. David left by the eastern gate. And he stopped by the edge of the city and watched while his troops moved past him to lead the way. The priests came too, carrying the Ark of God—and on the edge of the city they set it down beside the road until all the people went past. Then, "Take the Ark back into the city," David said quietly. "If the Lord sees fit, I'll come back and worship in the Tabernacle again. I'm leaving myself and all the people in His hands."

6. This means don't whine; just get in there and lick it.

And the priests—hup—hiked the poles back up on their shoulders and carried the Ark back into the city. Along with them, David sent two young men—Ahima-az and Jonathan.[7] "Keep your eyes open," he told them, "and your ears too. I'll stop at the ford of the Jordan River and wait there for a message from you. Let me know what happens in Jerusalem."

King David was using his head all right. But he still had a heart too. And it was breaking. He walked up to the Mount of Olives. His head was covered. And his feet were bare. And as he climbed the hill, he wept. The people who were with him were weeping, too, as a sign of mourning. It was as if the bottom of David's world had dropped out. His own son had rebelled against him, and many of his most faithful followers had deserted him. Even Ahithophel. "O Lord," David prayed as he climbed, "Ahithophel is advising Absalom right now. Confuse his mind, so he won't be able to do a good job of it. Please make him give Absalom foolish advice!"

He prayed as he walked on. And along with his prayer, he was thinking, "And who have I now to advise *me?*"

His answer was waiting for him at the top of the hill.

It was Hushai (Hew-shay-eye).

His head was covered, and he was weeping too. "What can I do to help?" he asked.

And all the pieces came together in David's mind. "You'll be no help if you come with me," he said. "Go back down the hill to Jerusalem. And when Absalom comes, tell him that you will be *his* servant. Tell him that you will be *his* adviser as you once were mine. Make him think that you have rebelled against me and turned to him."

"Yes, sire. And—?"

"Well, you can do two things. You can send messengers

7. This was *another* Jonathan.

84

and let me know what's going on. And you can confuse Ahithophel. Whatever he advises Absalom to do—confuse it—frustrate it."

"Yes, my king."

"Ahima-az and Jonathan are there as spies," David went on. "Tell them whatever Absalom finally decides to do, they will come and tell me."[8]

"Yes," said Hushai. And he bowed, then turned and hurried down the hill.

Hail the Conquering Hero!!??

That's what Absalom might have thought. He sailed into Jerusalem like the Queen Mary; all the others with him were merely tugboats. He was the big shot, and no mistake. Ahithophel was with him, as his adviser. And Hushai went immediately to see him.

"Long live the king!" said Hushai.

Well, *that* was a twist, Absalom thought. "Why aren't you with my father David?" he asked.

"That's easy," said Hushai. "I work for the top man. And you seem to be it."

And Absalom fell for it. Top man, eh? Well, he might as well finish the job he'd started. He sent for Ahithophel. "What shall I do now?" he asked.

"Easy," said Ahithophel. "Just give me twelve thousand men—I'll go out after David tonight."

"Why tonight?"

"Well, he's weary, he's discouraged, he's exhausted. His troops will be thrown into a panic. By morning they'll all be yours, signed, sealed and delivered."

It *did* look easy. Seemed to be good advice.

---

8. Trying to read all these men's names is like saying "fruit-float" fast five times. Just remember, their names might be hard to pronounce, but they were real, real people. And all this really happened. Don't let their names bother you!

It *was* good advice. And if Absalom had taken it, he would have won the day. But God was on David's side. Absalom hesitated. "Send for Hushai, my father's adviser—uh—my father's *ex*-adviser," he said.

And they did.

And they told him what the plans were.

But Hushai was using his head.

"Well?" said Absalom. "What do you think? Speak up!"

"Uhuh," said Hushai. "This time I think Ahithophel has made a mistake. You know your father and his men. They're mighty warriors. And right now they're probably as mad as a mother bear who's been robbed of her cubs."

Absalom pricked up his ears. He knew how fierce a warrior his father was.

"And your father's an old soldier," Hushai went on. "He's not going to be spending the night among his troops. He's probably already holed up in some cave. And he'll come out like a thunderbolt and throw your troops into panic. All he has to do is attack a few of them, and they'll all start shouting that your whole army is being slaughtered. Then even the bravest of them will be paralyzed with fear. They won't have a chance. Why, all of Israel knows what a mighty man your father is."

"What, then?" said Absalom. "What do *you* suggest?"

"Why, it's easy," said Hushai. "Just mobilize the entire army of Israel."

(Ah, this would take time.)

"Bring them from as faraway as Dan and Beer-sheba, so you'll have a huge force!"

(This would take a LOT of time.)

"And," said Hushai shrewdly, "I think you should personally lead the troops."

Absalom preened himself like a peacock.

"And when we find them, we can destroy his entire army," Hushai went on, warming to his subject, "so that not one of them is left alive. You'll have the armies of all Israel at your command." This was getting good. "And if David has escaped to some city, you can even take ropes and drag down the walls until they tumble into the nearest valley!"

Ah, what a picture. Absalom's eyes were gleaming. "That's what we'll do," he said. "That's *just* what we'll do."

He didn't know it, but he had just signed his own death warrant.

The Beginning of the End

Absalom issued orders to carry out Hushai's instructions. People got stuck in the doorways rushing to do his bidding. Absalom was busy getting ready for the big scene, to crush his father. But Hushai was busy too.

He sent the messengers—Ahima-az and Jonathan—to David. "Find him," he whispered, "and tell him not to stay at the Jordan River tonight. He must go at once into the wilderness. And hide there. I'll keep in touch with him."

The Stage Is Set

Hushai's instructions had been carried out to the letter. At last Absalom was ready. And that's what the problem was. *At last* he was ready. For, thanks to Hushai, it had taken him so long, that by the time he got to the Jordan, David and his army were safe in the city of Mahanaim (May-ha-*nay*-im) many miles away.

David had traveled to Mahanaim, gathering men and more men, like a rolling snowball gathers snow—till, by the time he got there, he had a sizable army. It wasn't as large as Absalom's army, but every last man was an experienced military man who had fought under David before. And David hadn't forgotten his experience either; he was still one of the greatest generals in the world.

He divided his men into three battalions, under the leadership of Joab, Abishai and Ittai (*Jo*-ab, A-*bish*-a-eye and *It*-ta-eye). Everything he was doing was right. Time was on his side. And God was on his side.

"You must not go into battle." David's men charged him. "You are worth ten thousand other men. You *have* to stay here in the city. You can give your orders from here. In here you'll be safe. We need you, King David."

David sighed and agreed. And gave the orders for the rest of them to go on. His heart was broken. And as they left, his troops heard him give his commanders this charge: "For my sake," he said, and his voice was trembling, "deal gently with young Absalom."

The Drama Begins

What a battle it was! It took place in the forest of Ephraim (Ee-fraw-im). Absalom and his men tore into David's army with great gusto. But David's generals tore into Absalom's army like a *tornado*—whirling, twisting, picking up and hurling down, and scattering the battle all over the whole country. And more men disappeared into the forest than the men who were killed!

The Drama Unfolds

Absalom put the brakes on his mule and brought him to a screaming stop. And he sat there, his eyes goggling out of his head, his mouth gaping open. His army had been pulverized. His dream of being king had been pulverized, too. And dead ahead of him—was a group of David's warriors!

He sat there paralyzed for a moment, his mule quivering beneath him. Then he jerked the mule around, digging his heels into its flanks—wham! And it ran pell-mell through the forest, absolutely terrified. The twigs snapped and the leaves crackled and the wind whistled through the boughs of the trees as they went wildly on. Absalom tried desperately to steer the mule as it fled blindly through any opening it could find, scrambling through brush and under low-hanging boughs.

Absalom hung on, his heart pounding so hard he thought it would leap out of his mouth. And then—

Ahhhhhhhhk!

His head was jerked back with such force he thought his neck had been broken. It was as if some giant hand had pulled him off the mule. Before he could realize what had happened, he was dangling in the air. His mule no longer was beneath him.

His mule was no longer beneath him!

It had run on ahead and disappeared into the brush. Absalom was disconnected from his perch. He was dangling in the air from the branch of an oak tree. And his hair—his beautiful long hair—was caught in the branches! He reached up frantically trying to disentangle it—but it would not come loose. And he swung there, helpless.

Through the blinding pain, he saw David's men coming toward him. They argued a moment, then one of them left in a trot. Disappeared in the woods. And came back with David's general, Joab.

The last thing Absalom saw was Joab, drawing three daggers.

And the Last Curtain Comes Down

Joab plunged the daggers into Absalom's heart. Then the armor bearers surrounded him—and finished him off. They threw him into a pit. And covered him with a great heap of stones. And then the trumpet was blown, for all of David's armies to hear.

It was all over.

The army disbanded. And the men went back to their homes.

Fall of a Big Shot—

Back in the city of Mahanaim, King David was seated at the gate. A watchman had climbed the stairs to his post at the top of the wall. The wait had been long and anxious, and they were both weary, when the watchman called out that he saw a messenger coming. And then another messenger.

David had been a great warrior all his life. But when the

89

messengers reached him, he did not ask how the battle was going. This day, more than anything else, he was a father.

"Is Absalom safe?" he asked.

They tried to break it to him gently. "Blessed be the Lord your God who has destroyed the rebels who dared to stand against you."

"But what of young Absalom? Is he all right?"

"Today Jehovah has rescued you from all those who rebelled against you."

"But what about my son? Is *he* all right?" David demanded.

They finally had to come out with it. "May all of your enemies be as that young man is!" they said.

That could mean only one thing.

Absalom was dead.

—Like a Tale That Is Told

The soldiers stood there in silence as David turned on his heel and climbed the stairs weeping. "O my son Absalom," he cried, "my son, my son Absalom. If only I could have died for you! O Absalom, my son, my son."

The drama was over. The sad tale had been told. Absalom had wanted to be a big shot, no matter who he stepped on, no matter who he hurt. Of all the people in the world, the one he hurt the most was his own father. And of all the people in the world, his father was the one who loved him the most.

What About You?

Can you think of times when you've wanted to be a big shot, no matter who you stepped on?

Make a list of the people you *have* stepped on, or you think you *might* have stepped on. Be honest, now. Don't fudge. Is it possible that the people you might have hurt the most were the people who loved you the most? Did you ever stop to think that the one you *really* hurt the most, is your Father in heaven?

I WISH
I HAD A REAL, TRUE FRIEND

CHAPTER 9/ 2 Samuel 15:17–37; 16:15–19; 17:1–22; 19:1–8

Well, you have plenty of company; everybody wishes that.

If you were to make a list of your real friends, how many would you have? We're not talking about just acquaintances; if you were to make a list of your acquaintances, you could fill pages. We're talking about real, true friends. Could you count them on both hands? One hand? Would you have four? Would you have two? One?

Well, if you've never thought it through before, how about making a list of the things you would *want* in a real true friend. What sort of a person would you want this friend to be?

Certainly in the fracas[1] David had with Absalom during those dark days of Absalom's revolt, he found out who his friends were.

There was Ittai (*It*-ta-eye).

1. It was a knock-down-drag-'em-out fight.

93

Ittai had been David's friend from *way* back. Remember when David had first run away from Saul and had fled to the Philistine city of Gath? And the rulers of Gath had cried, "Who needs him?"—and booted him out? Guess who followed him?

Ittai—and six hundred of his men.[2]

Yes, *sir*—Ittai had packed up and followed David out to the unknown—they didn't even know what lay ahead or where their next meal was coming from. And Ittai stuck with David through all those dark days—closer than a brother. And when David was finally made king and moved into Jerusalem, guess who was still with him?

Ittai.

And on that dark day when Jerusalem was evacuated and David stood at the gates and watched all the people go by—families, servants, soldiers—guess who he saw coming with them?

Ittai. Ittai, and his six hundred men.

David beckoned to Ittai to come over to where he was "What are you doing here?" he asked.

"I'm going to fight for you," Ittai said. "I'm on your side."

"But you're not one of my people," David said. "you don't have to fight for me. You are like my *guest* here in Jerusalem. Why should I ask you to risk your life for me?"

"I've vowed by God," Ittai said quietly, "that wherever you go, I'll go."

"No," said David, "go on back. Take your troops with you. And may the Lord be merciful to you."

"No, I'm going with you."

"We may be losers, Ittai."

"I go with you, David—whether it means life or death."

David looked at his friend for a moment. Then he sighed. "All right, come with us," he said.

Ittai signaled to his six hundred men and their families.

2. **They were known as Gittites.**

94

They picked up their duffle bags again, and trudged on down the road. Ittai walked off to join them. But before he got out of sight, he turned and made a signal to David. It was a "win or lose—I'm with you" sort of signal.

How do you suppose *he* stacked up as a friend?

Then of course there was Hushai (*Hew*-shay-eye).

He's the chap who met David at the top of the Mount of Olives on that same dreadful day.

His clothes were torn and there was dirt on his head, a sign of great distress.

He thrust out his hands to David as if to say, "What can I do to help?"

"You can be of more help to me—"

"Yes? Yes?"

"—if you go back down into the city." And David gave him his orders.[3]

Ooops.

This was asking Hushai to really stick his neck out. This meant he had to play a part in the camp of the enemy. He had to persuade Absalom that Ahithophel's advice was wrong. He had to persuade Absalom not to go after David. And convince him that it was better to wait until he had gathered the entire army of Israel.

Now that took a bit of doing. One slip-up, and Hushai was as good as dead. But he was willing to do it.

How do you suppose *he* stacked up as a friend?

And then there were Jonathan and Ahima-az. They were the two young men who brought the bulletins and the late bulletins and the late, late bulletins back to David. They were the ones who had to get to David somehow, and tell him not to wait at the Jordan River, but to get out of there as fast as he could.

It had all been so carefully planned. As soon as Hushai had any instructions for David, the plan was to be put into

3. You read them in the last chapter.

action. A maidservant was to be posted nearby. Hushai was to tell her. And she was to go tell the two young men who were hiding at En-rogel. And they were to go tell David. It was sort of a zigzag way to get word to David. And it was a very, very clever plan indeed. Except for one thing.

It didn't work.

No, it didn't work at all.

Hushai zigged the message to the maidservant all right. And the maidservant zagged the message to Jonathan and Ahima-az all right. But when *they* left their station to zig the message to David—

A boy saw them.

And he didn't zig and he didn't zag. He made a straight beeline back to Absalom and told him about it.

The jig was up.

Now Jonathan and Ahima-az could have deserted right then and there. They could have given up the whole business and left David to shift for himself. They could have just said, "Every man for himself!" and called it a day.

But they did not.

They were David's friends.

Now the Bible tells us that after they realized the lad had seen them, they both went away quickly. Which means they ran like mad. But they didn't run *away* from trouble.

No.

A while later, they came panting into the courtyard in the town of Bahurim (Bay-*hew*-rim). The man who lived there was one of David's supporters.

"Pssssst," they said.

"What's up?" asked the man.

"The jig is up, is what's up," they hissed, "unless you hide us. Quickly!" Their eyes darted around the little courtyard. Then they all saw it at once. A well.[4] The man motioned

---

4. It was a cistern cut in the rock; there was scarcely any water in it.

toward it. They let themselves over the side and scrambled in. The man's wife came running out of the house at the same moment. At a look from her husband, she quickly put a cover over the well. And spread some grain on it to dry in the sun. And went back into the house. The man pretended to putter around the courtyard. Then he went off to do some chores. Everything was quiet and undisturbed, as if no one had been there at all.

When Absalom's servants came to the house they saw nothing unusual. A woman about her work. Grain drying in the sun. Nothing unusual at all.

"Where are they?" asked Absalom's men.

"Where are who?" the woman said.

"David's men. Ahima-az and Jonathan," they said.

"Ahima-az and *Who*athan?" she said. "Oh—*those* men."

"Yes. *Those* men."

"Why, they—they've gone over that way—over the brook. They didn't say where they were headed. I have no idea." She wiped her hands on her apron and stood there fidgeting, waiting for them to go.

They stared at her a moment, then whirled around and ran. In a moment they were gone.

The little courtyard was silent for a long time.

Then, after a while, when she was sure they were well out of the way, she took the cover off the top of the well. And they came scrambling up.

"They went that way," she said. "Over the brook. When they don't find you they'll go back to Jerusalem. It's safe now for you to go on to King David."

And that is exactly what happened. The Bible tells us that when Absalom's men looked and looked and could not find the two young men, they returned to Jerusalem, their mission a failure. Ahima-az and Jonathan had apparently disappeared into thin air.

Meanwhile they were hurrying to the place where King David was hiding. "You'll have to go!" they blurted out. "You can't waste a minute!" And they told him the whole story. "Hushai said thus-and-thus and we did thus-and-thus—"

What they did *not* say was that Hushai had risked his life, and that they had indeed risked theirs. They had risked their lives for David when he was down-and-out.

How do you suppose *they* stacked up as friends?

And the upshot was (as you read in the last chapter) that David and his followers were safe in the city of Mahanaim before Absalom ever got to first base.

There were others. They are mentioned only in passing.[5]

But they had all done the same thing. They had stuck by David through thick and thin. They had supported him when the chips were down.

David had friends, all right. He had fair-weather friends. And then he had real, true friends who stuck with him when things were rough.

They were loyal to him even when they had to risk their lives.

How About You?

And while we're about it, how do *you* stack up? As a friend, that is.

Let's go back to this list of yours. After reading this chapter, would you like to go back and re-juggle and re-think it? What are the things you'd really like to have in a friend? What kind of a person would you want him (or her) to be?

After you have your list all squared away, stare at it for a minute, and think about it.

Now tack the list on the back of your closet door so you can see it often.

Now for the hard part.

Make up your mind that you are going to be that sort of a person *yourself*.

5. Second Samuel 18:27-29.

The greatest friend you will ever have in all your life—is Jesus.

"Henceforth I call you not servants; for the servant knoweth not what his lord doeth: but I have called you friends; for all things that I have heard of my Father I have made known unto you" (John 15:15, *KJV*).

If you are His friend, it means you'll be loyal to Him—when the going is smooth, and when the going is rough. Through thick and thin. It won't always be easy to be His friend. To be loyal to Jesus will cost you something.

How will *you* stack up?

I WISH
MY PARENTS WOULD STOP BUGGING ME

CHAPTER 10/ 1 Kings 1:5—2:12,34;
1 Chronicles 28:1-21; 29:23-25

"My Parents Won't Let Me Do Anything"

Are you squirming under discipline? Your parents are too strict for your comfort? And you wail, "All the others do it."

Yes, indeed.

Well, of course it depends on who "all the others" are and whether it is *really* "all the others" or just a *few*—and exactly what it is they're doing.

The dictionary says discipline means "teaching; training which *corrects.*" It sounds hard to take, and sometimes it is. Yaaak.

There was a letter in a newspaper once that said, "My parents won't let me do anything the other kids do. I have to be in early and they want to know where I'm going and who I'll be with and everything. Isn't it about time I got to do what I want to do without answering to them for everything?" And it was signed "Embarrassed."

More about that later.

There was a young man once who was working on a farm for the summer. The hours were long and the work was hard. And do you know who *his* parents were? Well, his father was Calvin Coolidge, the president of the United States!

What?

Yes. And I know what you're thinking. The boy's friends thought the same thing. "Man!" they said, "if my father were president I'd be off somewhere having a good time!"

And young Coolidge said, "You don't know my father."

But Isn't It Just for Ordinary Kids?

"What? Discipline for the son of a president? Isn't that just for ordinary kids? I thought sons of presidents and kings and people like that, could do just about as they pleased."

News for you.

Any young person who is brought up to do as he pleases is headed for trouble. *Any* young person. No matter who he is. Yes, even the sons of presidents. And the sons of kings.

There are all kinds of ways to be unpleasant in the classroom and in the school yard. But a spoiled brat can find more ways to be unpleasant than just about anybody else.

He is, sad to say, a crashing bore. And nobody wants to have anything to do with him. And whether he lives in a humble cottage or a palace, a spoiled brat is, sad to say, a spoiled brat.

Anatomy of a Spoiled Brat

There was one who lived back in the days of David. If he'd gone to public school he would have been voted the one most likely to grow up annoying people. But he didn't go to public school, for he was not an OK.[1] He was a KK.[2]

1. Ordinary kid.
2. King's kid.

Yes, he was one of David's own sons.

Chap by the name of Adonijah (Ad-o-*ny*-jah).

Now David was probably one of the greatest men the world has ever known. But he wasn't perfect. He did make a few mistakes. And some of them were dillies. And one of the biggest dillies he ever made, concerned Adonijah. For no matter what Adonijah did, David never scolded him. No matter what kind of mischief Adonijah got into, David never punished him. Adonijah was allowed to do exactly as he pleased. So before you could say, "Come with me to the woodshed," David had a spoiled brat on his hands.

Adonijah. Who else?

So, quite naturally, Adonijah considered himself to be his father's favorite. And also, quite naturally, he considered himself his father's presumptive heir.[3]

Who, after all, but David's spoiled child could be the new king when David died? And who, after all, was more qualified? Adonijah was handsome, he was a commanding figure, he was every bit as good-looking as Absalom had ever been (here we go again!). He was indeed all of these things, but as for his disposition—

Yaaak.

His oldest brother, Amnon, was dead. His next older brother, Chileab, was dead. And his *next* older brother, Absalom, was dead. And the next one was—Adonijah himself! Of course his kid brother was running around, but he didn't matter—or so Adonijah thought. He didn't matter at all. He was a chap by the name of Solomon. And who ever heard of *him?*

And so Adonijah dreamed his dreams and schemed his schemes.

Now making plans is one thing. But scheming mischief is quite another. Wait and see.

---

3. *He'd* get to be king.

Who Ever Heard of Solomon?

Now schemers of mischief come in a large assortment of shapes and sizes—good-looking and not-so-good-looking, bright and not-so-bright, tall, short, fat and thin. But they had one thing in common—sooner or later a schemer is bound to make a mistake. And one of the biggest mistakes Adonijah ever made was underestimating his kid brother. So in all his plans, he wasn't counting on the most important thing. God knew and David knew who the next king was going to be. And it was *not* Adonijah.[4]

"I Can Do Anything I Please"

While he was growing up, this was Adonijah's theme song. So it was quite natural for him to think to himself, "I will be king." And why not? He always did everything he wanted and got everything he wanted. So why not now? His father David was a very very old man. He was confined to his bed most of the time. It was time a new king took over. So Adonijah decided to crown himself.

The first thing he did was hire chariots and drivers. *Real fancy* chariots and drivers. Then he recruited fifty men to run down the street before him as royal footmen.[5]

The second thing he did was collect himself some followers to help him carry out this skulduggery.[6] He recruited Joab, the famous commander-in-chief of David's armies, and Abiathar (A-*by*-a-thar), one of David's priests. And he took them into his confidence and they agreed to help him.

(He didn't have much luck recruiting Zadok [*Zay*-doke] the priest and Benaiah [Bee-*nay*-iah] the head of David's personal bodyguards. He had no luck with the prophet Nathan either. Or with David's army chiefs.)

The next thing Adonijah did was stage and produce his

---

4. See 1 Kings 1:13 and 2 Samuel 7:12-16.
5. Do you remember who else did this? Remember how it turned out?
6. That means some hanky-panky was going on.

own coronation. The place was at the fountain of En-rogel, just southeast of Jerusalem. There he sacrificed sheep and oxen and fat young goats on a huge rock called the Serpent's Stone. And there he arranged a solemn feast.

He invited all the royal officials of Judah. But he did *not* invite Nathan the prophet. Or Benaiah. Or the army chiefs. And he invited all his brothers. But he did *not* invite brother Solomon.

And the next thing he did—
But more about that later.

"The Plot Is Thickening"

But this was not the only drama that was unfolding. There was another drama unfolding back at the palace.

A servant hurried to Solomon's mother Bathsheba (*Bath-sha-ba*), in the women's quarters. And announced an important visitor. The prophet Nathan was there to see her. It was urgent.

Nathan? To see her? Bathsheba was astonished. "Tell him to come in," she said.

He came in hurriedly. And wasted no time. There was no small talk. He got right to the point. "Do you realize that Adonijah has just staged his own coronation—has just announced himself a self-made king?"

"Adonijah!?"

"Yes. He's staging his own coronation this very minute. And David doesn't even know about it."

Bathsheba turned pale. It was the custom in those days for a new king to have all his rivals killed. And her son, Solomon, would certainly be considered rival number one.

"If you want to save your life," Nathan went on, as if he could read her thoughts, "and the life of your son, Solomon— do exactly as I say." He whispered hurried instructions. And Bathsheba listened. Their heads were close together, their faces pale.

Moments later, Bathsheba was ushered into King David's bedroom.

He was an old, old man now, attendants waiting on him, and nurses caring for him.

Bathsheba bowed low before him.

"What do you want?" he asked.

She got right to the point. "My lord," she said, "you vowed to me by the Lord your God that our son, Solomon, would sit upon your throne."

"Yes?"

"But instead, Adonijah proclaimed himself the new king. And you did not even know about it."

David stared at her in disbelief.

"It's true," she said. "He is celebrating his coronation. He has sacrificed oxen and sheep and goats. He invited Abiathar the priest."

"Abiathar?"

"Yes. And Joab too. And all your sons. But he did not invite Solomon. My lord the king, all Israel is awaiting your decision as to whom you have chosen to succeed you. If you don't act now, Solomon and I will be killed. We'll be arrested and executed as criminals as soon as—"

"Nathan the prophet is here to see you, sire," one of the king's aides had broken in. Bathsheba bowed low and backed away. She had been expecting this. It was part of her instructions.

A moment later, Nathan came in right on cue and bowed before the king. "My lord, have you appointed Adonijah to be the next king? Is he the one to sit on your throne and rule Israel?"

David stared.

"Well, today," Nathan went on, "he celebrated his coronation. He invited your sons to attend the festivities. He also invited Joab and Abiathar the priest. They are feasting and drinking with him right now at En-rogel. They're shouting 'Long live King Adonijah!'"

David just listened, propped up on his pillows. His face was a big question.

"Those of use who are loyal to you were not invited," Nathan went on. "Zadok the priest. And Benaiah. And Solomon and I. None of us was invited. Did you know about this? And what will you do about it? You haven't yet said a word about who will be the next king."

At last David spoke. "Call Bathsheba back," he said.

Bathsheba was waiting for *her* cue. She came back in immediately and stood before the king.

"Bathsheba?" David said.

"Yes, my lord."

"I decree that our son, Solomon, will be the next king and will sit upon my throne. Just as I swore by God to you before."

"Thank you, sire," said Bathsheba, bowing low again. "May my lord the king live forever."

"Call Zadok the priest," said David. "And call Nathan back. And tell the servants to get Benaiah."

Later they all stood around his bed and waited for him to speak. He strained forward on his pillows, holding himself up on his elbows. The late afternoon sun filtered in through the windows and shone upon his face and on his hair. His hair was white now, and his face was pale. But his eyes were bright and glowing, and for a moment—just for a moment—the grand old man seemed strangely young again. All the old fire was there, and the passion, and the enthusiasm, and the hopes and the dreams were there. He seemed like the ruddy-faced boy with the beautiful red hair who had played his harp for Saul so many years before. For one brief moment he was absolutely in command again. He issued his orders and gave his instructions. Though his voice trembled, the orders were crisp. And they had the zing and the air of authority about them that had always overwhelmed people, all during his reign.

Everyone snapped to attention. And then scattered to do his bidding.

What happened after that echoed and re-echoed all over—all over Jerusalem and all over the countryside.

They heard it in Jerusalem and they danced in the streets. And they heard it at En-rogel.

Solomon and his brothers heard it. And King David and his other sons heard it. And the officials that had been invited to the coronation heard it. And General Joab heard it. And Abiathar the priest heard it—

And Adonijah heard it.

They were just finishing their coronation banquet.

"What's all the commotion?" Adonijah demanded. "What is the shouting? What is the singing?"

"Yes—what's going on?" asked Joab. "Why is the city in such an uproar?"

While he was still speaking, Jonathan, the son of Abiathar the priest rushed in. "Come over!" Adonijah said. "You must have good news! Has everyone heard of my coronation? Does everyone know that I've declared myself king? Is that what they're rejoicing about? Come over, come over!"

But Jonathan did not take another step. He shouted from where he was standing. "Our lord King David has declared Solomon to be king!"

Everyone gaped, silent.

"The king sent him with Zadok the priest to Gihon."[7]

Their eyes boggled.

"Yes, the king sent him to Gihon with Zadok and Nathan and Benaiah!"

"Whaaaa—?"

Adonijah dropped his wine flask.

"And he rode on the king's own mule! The mule that no one but a king is allowed to ride on!"

"But—!" Adonijah's mouth sagged open.

---

7. Gihon was a rocky cliff on the south side of Jerusalem in the Kidron valley. In the rock was a cave, with a fountain that supplied Jerusalem with water. It must have looked like a beautiful theater for Solomon's coronation!

"And Zadok and Nathan have anointed him the new king of Israel!"

Auuuuuuuuugh.

Adonijah began to scramble to his feet.

"They had just returned. The whole city is celebrating! That's what the noise is all about!"

Adonijah stood there, swaying back and forth as if his spine had turned to jelly.

"Yes! Solomon is sitting on the throne and all the people are congratulating King David on his choice. And they're calling God's blessing down on him. And he's lying in bed, acknowledging their blessings. And he's saying, 'Thank You, Lord, for putting Solomon on my throne while I'm still alive to see it!'"

The fires under the sacrifices had stopped crackling. The places where they had been were smoking and silent. The men who had been feasting with Adonijah had got to their feet by now. And they just stood there, gaping. All their hopes and all their plans and all their dreams were shattered. They looked at the half-dead fires as if all their plans and all their dreams were going up in the smoke.

Then, as if someone had given them a cue, they scattered in all directions and disappeared. Each man went his own way. They were absolutely terrified.

Adonijah stood there a moment and looked at the remains of the banquet, and the smoke curling up.

The food was eaten, the fires were dead, his plans were dead—

Then suddenly he bolted into action.

Why, *he* was as good as dead too!

His scheme hadn't worked!

After the terrible thing he had done, Solomon would kill him, unless—unless—

The Tabernacle! He'd be safe in the Tabernacle! Anyone who went to the Tabernacle and clung to the altar of God—was safe!

No one would dare harm him!
Panic! Horrors! Got to get to the altar! Quickly! HELP!

"I Didn't Know It Would Come to This"

A few minutes later, he had flung himself into the Tabernacle and knelt at the altar of God, gasping for breath. He grabbed the huge horns at the corners of the altar. And his body sagged, as he collapsed against it, panting, hanging on for dear life.

The priests that were on duty at the Tabernacle stood there silently, watching him.

"Will the King Solomon swear to me—"

King Solomon. Ha!

"Will the King Solomon swear to me that he won't kill me with the sword?"

One of the priests signaled silently to a servant, gave a whispered order, and the servant left. A few moments later, he came back and brought his answer to the priest. The priest touched Adonijah on the shoulder. "King Solomon has sent for you," he said quietly. "He will not harm you—"

Adonijah looked up, unbelieving. His face was streaked with tears and soot.

"He will not harm you," the priest went on, "if you behave yourself. He wants to see you. Now begone."

Adonijah let go of the horns of the altar and let them help him to his feet. His knees were stiff. He walked like a mechanical toy, in a daze, toward the palace. A moment later he was ushered into Solomon's presence. Solomon was no longer his kid brother; Solomon was the new king of Israel.

Adonijah bowed low before the king. They looked at each other for a moment. And then Solomon nodded toward the door.

"Go on home," he said.

That was all.

The interview was over.

Ouch!

Adonijah backed out of the room as fast as his stiff knees would let him. And bowed. A moment later he was shuffling across the courtyard, on his way back to his own house.

All his "well-wishers" were gone. The cheering section had disappeared. He was a picture of a chap who had got his own way all his life.

What About You?

Remember that letter in the beginning of this chapter? It was signed "Embarrassed."

Well, a few weeks later another letter appeared in the same newspaper. And it said: "This is an answer to 'Embarrassed.' Tell him or her to thank God for parents like that. My parents didn't care what I did. They didn't care where I was or who I was with. There was no law in our house—I did just as I pleased. And when I got into little scrapes they bailed me out and let me go on my merry way. Well now I'm in *real* trouble and there's no bailing me out. I wish my parents had cared enough to clamp down before it was too late." And it was signed "Embittered."

Down in your heart, you *want* somebody to care enough about you to discipline you.

Don't you, now?

"For whom the Lord loveth he chasteneth . . ." (Heb. 12:6).

You see, if your parents won't discipline you, the Lord will.

So you might as well get one jump ahead, and:

"Children, obey your parents in the Lord . . ." (Eph. 6:1).

THE BEST
WISH OF ALL

CHAPTER 11/ 1 Chronicles 28:1–21;
1 Kings 3:1–28; 4:29–34; 9:26—10:29; 2 Chronicles 1

If You Really Had a Wish . . .

Well, let's just try it on for size. Suppose you really *did*
have three wishes.

There was a little boy once (and of course this isn't a true
story; it's just a little story from a child's paint book) who
spent most of his time wishing for things he didn't have. He
used up so much time wishing, that he didn't have any time
left to take care of his everyday living or to tackle most of
his problems. He grew very lazy.

Well, one day, as the story goes, the boy was sitting under
an apple tree, doping off,[1] when who should appear out of
the thin air, but a chubby fairy. Yes, she was as round as
a butterball. And she told him, of all things, that he could
have anything he wished for all that day, BUT. He couldn't
take back any wish, once it was made.

1. What else? Wishers are great doper-offers.

113

And then she was gone.

Now, although this boy had never been much good in facing up to his problems, he was very good at wishing: he had had a lot of practice. So he was very quick to catch on. Right away he wished for a huge dish of ice cream. And before you could say, "Make mine fudge ripple," there it was. Right in his lap. He promptly ate it, and then remembered that he had to go to a birthday party that afternoon. So he wished himself home. Sure enough, in one big *S-W-O-O-P*, he was home in his own room. And there were his clothes laid out, and his mother was calling up from downstairs for him to hurry.

And there's where his wishing went to his head.

First he couldn't get into his shoes. But instead of loosening the laces, he grumbled, "I wish these shoes were three times as big."

Oh, oh.

There they were, suddenly as big as shoe boxes.

"Oh, boy," he muttered. "What'll I do? Wear my sneaks. Maybe nobody will notice."

And then things began to go uncomfortably from bad to worse. "Better put my suit on. And my shirt. Where's my shirt? Um. Umph. Hup. Mmmm. Oh, brother. I can't get this buttoned. Crazy buttons. Why won't this button? Buttons. Yaaak. I wish there were no such things as buttons. I wish—Oh, brother. I shouldn't have said that."

Yes. You guessed it.

No buttons.

Well, he got himself together with pins and paper clips and Scotch tape and whatever else he could find. And started to comb his hair. "Crazy hair. Must have slept on it the wrong way. Won't stay down. Rats. I didn't just sleep on it the wrong way. It *grows* the wrong way. I was *born* with it the wrong way. Stupid hair. I wish I didn't have any hair to comb—

"Wait a minute. I didn't mean that. I take it back. I didn't mean it. I'm afraid to look—

114

"Oh, brother. I'm as bald as a doorknob. I'd better wish I was back under the apple tree while I still have a head left."

And, sure enough, there he was.

"Now. I'm going to wish for a million dollars. And then tell that fairy to go someplace else and peddle her wishes." And he shouted up into the air, "I wish for a million dollars, fairy. Right now!"

Yep. A silver dollar landed right by his side. Oops. Then another. Plink. Another. Plink, plink. More. And more. Now they were coming fast. Ouch. Silver dollars were heavy. Now they were—whooops—now they were coming like mad. They were landing on his head. All over him. He was being buried in them. Up to his chest. Up to his neck. "Help! Please! Fairy!" In a minute they'd be over his head. "Fairy! FAIRYYYYY!"

And there she was, standing on a silver dollar, over his head.

"Have you had enough?" she asked.

"Save me, please!"

"Will you promise to stop your idle wishing and get down to business, living your life as it is?"

"Yes, yes! If you'll just put my hair back and make my shoes the right size and give me back my buttons, I'll never make any dumb wishes again!"

"All right. And just to make sure you've learned your lesson, I'm going to give you a sharp rap on your head with my trusty wand. Upppp! There!"

"Ouch! Not so hard!"

"And THERE!"

"Ouch! I'll never—

"Hey. Where am I? I've been dreaming! But what hit me? When she hit me on the head, it really hurt.

"Oh, oh." And then he looked sheepish and then he scrambled to his feet. What had hit him on the head had been an apple.

And at the story's end, he had stalked off. And for all

115

we know he had given up his idle wishing from there on out.

Foolish? Perhaps. It's a likely story for a coloring book. But for a moment—just for a moment, let's take this business of wishing seriously. Suppose you *could* have any wish you wanted?

What would you do?

There was a man once, who actually did get that chance. Really.

That man was Solomon.

Now suppose—just for a moment—

"This Is Too Heavy for Me—I Can't Handle It"

"But I can't identify with Solomon. It's ridiculous. He didn't have any problems. He already had everything he wanted. My problems are very real. And some of them I can't handle."

All right. We'll go along with that. We'll take you right where you are, in your own situation.

So what's your first problem?

"I'm Only a Kid Brother"[2]

"Actually I'm not very important in my family. All my brothers and sisters are older than me. And frankly I don't get along too well with any of them. Sometimes my older brothers and sisters—and life itself—seem to overwhelm me. I don't think I can handle it."

Well, you're not much different than Solomon, so far. He was a kid brother. And all his brothers hated him. His brother Adonijah would have killed him if he'd had the chance. But suddenly David had given the orders, and Solomon had been whisked off to Gihon and anointed with oil and proclaimed the next king of Israel. So that one moment he was a kid brother, and the next moment life *overwhelmed* him. And while all Jerusalem was rejoicing and singing and congrat-

2. Or kid sister, as the case may be.

ulating him, he must have been shivering in his sandals,
wondering if he could handle it, too.

It was pretty heavy business.

"My Parents Expect Too Much of Me"

"Really, some of the things my parents expect of me, you
just wouldn't believe. I have talks with my dad about what
he expects me to do, and to be—that leave my head spinning.
They expect too much and sometimes I worry about whether
I'm going to be able to live up to it."

Well, Solomon had that little problem too.

For a while after he was made king, he ruled Israel *with
his father David.* But David was a very old man. So the time
came, and all too soon, when he summoned all his officials
and political leaders—everybody in authority in his kingdom,
and gave them what we'd call a farewell address. He told
them how he had wanted to build a temple where the Ark
of God could rest. And how he had collected everything
necessary for the building. And how the Lord had told him
that he was *not* the man chosen to build it.

Then he dropped the bombshell.

"Solomon," he said, turning to his son, "the Lord has chosen
you to build His holy temple. Be strong and do as He com-
mands."[3]

Too much!

Then David gave Solomon the blueprint of the Temple
and its surroundings. And he weighed out gold and silver
for every single thing in it. "Every part of this blueprint,"
he told Solomon, "was given to me in writing from the Lord.

"Now all you have to do is build it."

Heavy business indeed.

"Why Couldn't You Give Me Something Easy?"

"I'm just not up to the jobs my parents—and my teach-

3. See 1 Chronicles 28:10 (*TLB*).

ers—give me to do. If they'd give me easy stuff that I could just do with my hands tied behind my back, I could do it in a hurry and get back to my fun. But the jobs I get assigned to me! They call them 'projects'. But giving them a fancy name doesn't help. Sometimes I balk and they think I'm lazy—but I'm actually scared that I'm not going to be able to do them right."

Know what you mean. Read on, read on.

The more David told the people about that Temple, the more Solomon's head whirled. The size of it! The details! A million things to remember! And the costly things that would go into its construction! Gold—silver—bronze—iron—wood (good grief, where would he get the wood?)—precious stones, costly jewels—

Oh, *brother*.

"In addition to all the things I've collected," David went on, "I am giving all my own private treasures—a hundred million dollars' worth."

Too much!

"Now who will follow my example and give himself and all that he has to the Lord?"

Do you know, the pledges came in to the tune of more than a hundred and seventy-five *million* dollars—and over five thousand tons of bronze and iron, and jewelry like you wouldn't believe?!?[4]

Out of sight!

You're scared? How do you think *Solomon* felt?

When David had to tell Solomon to buck up—in several different ways, all in one sentence—[5]

"Be strong—

"Be of good courage—

"Fear not—

4. If your church is having a building program, you might tell them this. Could stick a pin in them and get them going!
5. See 1 Chronicles 28:20 (*KJV*).

118

"Don't be dismayed—

"God will be with you—

"He won't fail you—

"He won't forsake you—"

You can guess that Solomon must have been very wobbly-kneed indeed.

"But It's Worse than It's Ever Been Before"

"Right now, in my life, the responsibilities people have given me are more than I can bear. The things I'm expected to tackle by myself are too much for me. It's harder now than it's ever been before. Sometimes I wish I *could* be the little guy in the paint book, sitting under an apple tree, wishing for dishes of ice cream. I wish life were as *simple* as that."

You think Solomon didn't feel the same way?

After his father, David, died, the job before him was overwhelming. Suddenly he was *it*. The king of all Israel! His father had not only expected him to build a temple to the Lord, but had told all the people about it, and had even given him the plans for it. There was no backing down. And he had enemies, including his own brothers, who would have skinned him alive if given half a chance. There was probably no other person in the world at that time as young as he was who had a job as big as his to do.[6] Problems? All kinds of problems. You name it, and he had it. Any king kind of a problem you could think of, he had.

"What Do You Do When You're Surrounded by Problems?"

What do you do? Well, there was a chap once who was in the hospital surrounded by problems. Matter of fact, he was surrounded by a cast. Actually he was *in* it—up to his eyeballs. And a friend came to visit him and said, "How

6. He was only about nineteen or twenty years old.

119

long are you going to be *in* that thing?" And the chap answered. "A day at a time."

And that's the way to treat your problems. Stay very close to God. and tackle them one at a time. Meanwhile it's a pretty good idea to go about your business and do the next job at hand. This is the way Solomon went about it.

The first thing he did was weed out the people in his court who might be his enemies. This strengthened Israel from the inside. Then he made an alliance with Egypt, his most powerful neighbor,[7] which strengthened Israel on the *outside*. So you might say Solomon strengthened Israel inside and out. He did a pretty thorough job of it.

The next thing he did was gather all his army officers and his political and religious leaders and take them up the hill to Gibeon where the old Tabernacle was. It was the original Tabernacle that had been carried all through the wilderness back in the days of Moses. And it had been at Gibeon for a long, long time. It was empty now, but the old bronze altar was still there in front. And Solomon and all those he had invited worshiped God and thanked Him for what He had done. The smoke from a thousand burnt offerings rose to the sky!

They camped there in Gibeon that night, and Solomon went to bed feeling that he was off to a good start. All day long he'd been watching the smoke of a thousand sacrifices rise to the Lord. And all day long, the One who was uppermost in his mind—was the Lord. And now as he lay on his makeshift bed at camp, he was still thinking of the Lord. Had not his father David written, "Lie quietly on your bed in silent meditation.[8] Put your trust in the Lord, and offer him pleasing sacrifices. . . . I will lie down in peace and sleep, for though

___

7. Actually, he married the Pharaoh's daughter, which caused him considerable trouble later on. You can read about it in the book, *The Strangest Thing Happened.*
8. Deep thinking.

I am alone, O Lord, you will keep me safe. . . ."[9]

Well, David was gone now, and Solomon was alone. And he needed the Lord now more than ever before.

He drifted off to sleep.

And that's when it happened.

"Do Things Like This Really Happen?"

"Ask me for anything, and I will give it to you."

What? What was this?

"Ask me for anything, and I will give it to you."

He'd been thinking of the Lord all day—and now the Lord had appeared to him in a dream!

Talk about getting your wishes! He could have anything he wanted!

What to wish for? That his enemies were all dead? That he had a chance to get even? That his problems would end? That he could worship God *his* way? What? *What?*

Wish, man, *wish!*

And Solomon did.

He asked for what had been on his mind all day. "O God," he said. "You have made me king over a nation so great that there are almost too many people to count. And right now I feel like a little child who doesn't know his way around. Give me an understanding mind so I can rule these people well. And so I can know the difference between what is right and what is wrong. For who is able to govern such a great nation as this one of Yours? I just can't do it all by myself."

Wisdom!

Solomon had asked for wisdom!

And the Lord was pleased.

"Because you have asked for wisdom in governing My people, and you haven't asked for a long life or riches for yourself, and you haven't asked Me to curse your enemies—

"Yes! I'll give you what you asked for! I'll give you a wiser

9. See Psalm 4 (*TLB*).

121

mind than anyone else has ever had before or will ever have again! And that's not all. I'll give you what you did *not* ask for—such riches and wealth and honor as no other king has ever had before you! And there will never again be so great a king in all the world!"

Glory be, wowee, and hallelujah!

Solomon got his wish, and much, MUCH more besides!

It was almost too good to be true!

But it *was* true.

Solomon went back down from that Tabernacle and back to Jerusalem. And he walked into the Tent-Tabernacle that David had constructed. And he stood before the Ark of God. And he offered sacrifices—and worshiped.

Then he invited all of his officials to a great banquet.

This was the beginning of a new life. He was never to be the same again.

A Wish Fulfilled—and Then Some!

Did God ever keep His promise! It was as if Solomon had held up a bucket and asked God to fill it to the top—and it got filled—piled up, pressed down, and running over!

Talk about wealth!

Solomon owned fourteen hundred chariots. And he had forty thousand chariot horses to pull them. And twelve thousand charioteers to drive them!

Why, the amount of food for the palace was staggering. A hundred and ninety-five bushels of flour. Three hundred and ninety bushels of meal. Ten oxen. Twenty pasture-fed cattle. A hundred sheep. To say nothing of deer and gazelles and roebucks and plump fowl. Groceries for a month? No— groceries for *one day!*

Expensive cedar lumber—the very best—was used like common sycamore. And silver and gold were as plentiful in Jerusalem as rocks on the roads!

And the building and trading and big business that went on was greater than the world had ever seen before!

And talk about wisdom!

Solomon was wiser than all the wise men of the East, including those in Egypt. He wrote three thousand proverbs[10] and one thousand songs. He knew practically all there was to know about animals and birds and snakes and fish. And growing things—from the great cedars of Lebanon down to the tiny hyssop that grew out of the cracks in the walls. He knew their habits and their growth patterns. He knew what made them tick and how they grew—he almost seemed to speak their language.

His fame spread throughout the world. And kings from other countries sent their ambassadors to him, to ask for his advice.

Wisdom in Action

All the tales of Solomon's wisdom could probably fill a ten-foot shelf in a library. But the most well-known tale of all is the one about the two women and their babies.

It happened like this:

There were two women who lived in the same house. And they each had tiny babies, born just three days apart.

It was in the deep, dark hours of the night that the dreadful thing happened. One of the women stirred in her sleep, then woke with a start. Something was wrong. She felt in the bed alongside her, trembling. Then she knew. She had rolled over on her baby, while she was sleeping. And she had smothered it. The child was dead! She lay there for a few minutes in shock and horror. Then she got up—ever—so—quietly—

And picked up her baby—

And tiptoed across the room to the other woman's bed—

And carefully—very carefully—

Put her *dead* baby alongside the other woman.

And picked up the other woman's *live* baby—

And carried it back to her own bed.

10. A true saying, a sort of a motto.

123

The little house was silent. And then—

The *other* woman stirred in her sleep. She went to cuddle her baby—and drew back in terror. The child was dead! She lay there trembling, holding the baby close and weeping quietly, until the first streaks of light stole across her bed. It got lighter. And lighter. She held the baby away from her a bit and looked into its little face. And then she sat up in bed, screaming—

"This is not my baby!!!"

Later that day, among the people to be judged at the court of King Solomon, were the two women—quarreling fiercely—and each one carrying a tiny baby. When their turn came they marched up the magnificent steps leading to the throne—or leaped up would be a better term, for they were like two tigers fighting over their cubs. Each one was intent on being heard.

"Sire, we live in the same house, just the two of us. And just recently our babies were born—three days apart," began the first woman. "But her baby died in the night when she rolled over and smothered it—"

"I did not!"

"—and smothered it, and she got up in the night and took my son from me and left her son beside me while I was sleeping—"

"She lies!"

"—and left her dead baby—"

"She lies! The dead baby is hers!"

"It is not! The living baby is mine and the dead baby is hers!"

"I know my own baby, you—!"

"And I know *my* own baby! The dead baby is yours!!!"

"Wait!"

It was King Solomon speaking. He'd heard enough. Everyone was suddenly silent.

124

"Wait just a minute," Solomon went on. "I can't hear you when you both speak at once."

Silence.

"Let's get the facts straight." The king was looking from one woman to the other. "This woman says the live child is mine and yours is dead. And this woman says no, the dead child is yours—my son is the living one."

Silence in the great court. And then, the king spoke.

"Bring me a sword."

It was as if a shiver went through the whole judgment hall. Mouths fell open. Eyeballs boggled.

"Cut the living child in half," the king said, "and divide it. And give half to one, and half to the other."

The whole crowd sucked in its breath at once.

A big, burly guard took the tiny baby and laid it on its little belly across his huge hand. He cupped his hand around it and held it aloft as it wiggled and squirmed.

Then he raised his sword and took careful aim.

All eyes were on that wiggling baby. All but the king's. Solomon was watching the faces of the two women. The guard drew his arm back, back, back—

And stopped.

One of the women had fallen to her knees. "No—no!" she screamed. "My lord, give her the living baby—don't kill him, please don't kill him!" And she sank to the floor sobbing.

But the other woman stood, her head high, her eyes narrowed. "Divide it!" she said. "It shall be neither mine *nor* yours. Divide it!"

Then the king knew.

"Wait!" he said to the guard. "Hold it."

This time the whole crowd let *out* its breath at once.

The guard dropped his sword to his side.

The king gestured toward the sobbing woman. "Give her the living child," he said, "and don't kill it. She is its mother."

Phew!

You'd better believe *that* was a day nobody ever forgot.

125

Especially the two women!

Word of Solomon's decision spread throughout the kingdom. And were people impressed? They were *awed.* [11]

Because they realized that the *wisdom of God was in him.*

Solomon had wished the best wish of all.

What About You?

Can you find ways in which Solomon's problems were a lot like yours? Everybody grows up under some pressures. Make a list of *your* pressures. Now make a list of *his.* Match them up. Any similarity?

How do you figure Solomon knew which was the real mother of the living baby? The one who didn't want it killed would have lost it anyway; she told Solomon to give it to the other woman rather than kill it. So how could he tell?

Do you think you could be trusted to get any wish you wanted? It could be dangerous business; sometimes the worst thing that can happen to you is getting what you want. It sort of depends on what you want, doesn't it?

What Is Wisdom Anyhow? And Who Needs It? And How Do You Get It?

Are you ready?

Wisdom is the ability to take a bunch of facts that you learn. And mesh them, or *put them in gear* with your own life. *And put them into action.* If you read a book on honesty and understand it—that's *knowledge.* But if you read a book on honesty and say, "Hey, that means *me!*" And you put it in action in your own life—that's *wisdom.*

Now there is *earthly* wisdom and *heavenly* wisdom. If you read a book on "How to Be Nasty in Ten Easy Lessons" and put it in action in your own life, you'll be headed for Nothingsville with no return ticket.

It's *heavenly* wisdom God wants you to have. And the Bible

11. They were bowled over with wonder and respect.

126

tells us that heavenly wisdom is pure. And gentle. And filled with kindness. And brave. And definitely *not phony*.[12]

And who needs it? Well, Solomon said, "Wisdom is better than rubies; and all the things that may be desired are not to be compared with it" (Prov. 8:11, *KJV*).

And how do you get it? "If any of you lack wisdom, let him ask of God, that giveth to all men liberally, and upbraideith not; and it shall be given him" (Jas. 1:5, *KJV*). Which means God will give you wisdom if you ask Him for it. And He won't scold you, either, or call you stupid.

Try it! It's the only way to go!

---

12. See James 3:13-17 (*TLB*).

THE WISH
COMES TRUE—
AND MORE SO!

The climax!

The peak!

The very top!

The most important day in Israel's history!

The Temple!

David had prepared for it—

He had gathered materials—lumber and limestone and iron and brass and gold and silver. And he had gathered work-men—stonecutters and carvers and dyers and craftsmen.[1] And he had even purchased the land—Mount Moriah, the very spot where Abraham had offered up his son Isaac to God, so many years before.

Everything was ready.

All the pieces were there.

They just had to be put together.

---

1. He had made a deal with King Hiram of Tyre to get these things.

129

"This is the beginning," he had said to Solomon. "Something to start with. And you have many skilled stonemasons and carpenters and craftsmen of every kind. So get to work, and may the Lord be with you!"

And Solomon had carried on from there.

One year, two years—

Lumber and cedar and cypress wood came by water and by land from King Hiram. Loggers got to work—and carpenters, and men in the stone quarries.

Three years, four years—

Thousands and thousands of men worked in relays[2]—

Four years—

Huge stones were cut to size in the quarries and lugged slowly and painfully to the building site—there to be fitted together without tools of any kind. No hammers. No nails.

Silently, silently—

Five years—

The Temple rose into the air. What a picture!

Outside—white stone, gleaming in the sunlight—complete with outer courts and pillars and porch. Inside—cedar wood paneling, completely covered with gold—with beautiful palm trees and flowers and angels carved on it. And when the light streamed in from the high windows and touched the gold—

Dazzling!

Six years—

Altars of brass and gold were fashioned—and golden basins and lampstands and tables and bowls and pots and shovels—

And two huge carved angels, their wings outspread, wingtip to wingtip and *wall to wall*—overlaid with gold.

Seven years—

Finished!

The great day had arrived!

---

2. Each group worked for a month and then came home for two months to work in their fields.

The Feast of the Tabernacles![3] And the Temple dedication! All rolled into one!

On every road leading into Jerusalem there was a gigantic traffic jam. And *in* Jerusalem? Standing room only!

The procession was carefully planned and went without a hitch. It started at the tent that David had built for the Ark of God years before. Solomon had invited the leaders of Israel for the ceremony. And as they watched, the priests put the poles through the rings in the Ark and carefully hoisted it up on their shoulders. Then they started through the streets of Jerusalem.

There were trumpets—
And cymbals—
And harps—
And psalteries—
And choirs! Great choirs!

The music rose to the heavens! All the way to the Temple!

The Temple area was absolutely *jammed* with people—wall to wall. They crowded back upon each other to get out of the way and let the procession through. The priests carried the precious Ark through the huge outer court, then up the steps to the priests' court where the great brass altar was, and the ENORMOUS bronze basin resting on twelve bronze oxen. There they set the Ark down. And so many sheep and oxen were sacrificed that they could not be counted.

When this was done, the priests picked up the Ark again and carried it into the Temple proper.

The people waited outside.

Inside, the priests carried the Ark through the holy place, with its golden lampstands and tables and altar of incense—
Up the steps—
Into the golden room, the holy of holies—
And very carefully lowered the precious Ark—

3. This was an annual feast of thanksgiving in October.

131

And set it down under the sheltering wings of the huge golden angels.

And then they turned to leave.

And then—

Light! Blinding light! Dazzling light!

It was a cloud—so bright it is impossible to describe—and it was filling the entire Temple!

The priests hurried outside, dazed, unable to finish their ceremony.

IT WAS THE GLORY OF THE LORD!

The word spread in whispers, through the court of the priests, through the outer court, then through the streets. For one brief beautiful moment, Almighty God Himself had come down—and His very presence had been right there in the Temple.

People were still breathless when Solomon stood to face them in the priests' court outside.

He stood before the huge bronze altar—

And raised his hands to heaven—

And a great hush fell over the crowds as he began to pray.

"O Lord God," he said. "This Temple has been built for You. And You've promised to live in it! But is it possible that God would really live on earth? Why, even the highest heavens cannot hold You!

"Hear the prayers of Your people—"

This meant the Israelites.

But there was more.

"And when *strangers* hear of Your great name and Your mighty miracles, and they worship You and pray to You—

"Hear *them* and answer *their* prayers!"

How *about* that?

This meant YOU!

"For," Solomon went on, "*all the nations of the earth* will know Your name just as Your own people do."

And now, today, three thousand years later—it's true! We

know His name and His miracles—and more! For we know somebody they didn't know—

Jesus.

God himself became a man and lived among us. And we do not offer sacrifices as they did in the Temple, for Jesus became the perfect sacrifice for us when He died on the cross.

And we don't look for Him to live in a Temple. We have a much much better arrangement than that.

He will live in your heart, in your very personality, in your life—if you'll ask Him.

For He has promised.

And you'd better believe it. For one other thing Solomon said later on in that prayer was—

"Not one word has failed of all His wonderful promises. . . ."

Your wish can come true—and more so!

CHAPTER 13/ 1 Kings 10:1-13

"It's great to hear all about the wisdom of God, and all His miracles, and things like that. But that all happened way back in the days of David and Solomon. I'd sure like to see some of those things for myself."

Now that's a very good point for you to bring up. You're a real thinker.

There was a woman once who felt the same way. She wasn't satisfied with just *hearing* about the things of God. She wanted to see for herself.

Ever hear of the Queen of Sheba? Did you think she was some sort of character in a storybook, like Long John Silver or Cinderella?

No—she was for real.

She was actually the queen of a country called Sheba. And Sheba was way down in the southern part of Arabia. It was a little strip of land stretched along the southwest coast, with the sea on one side, and on the other side—desert; and more

135

desert. And *more* desert. Miles and miles of it, endless dunes and trackless wastes—a great sea of sand.

What a place to live!

But the Queen of Sheba was not down there sitting in a tent with sand blowing in her soup. Not on your life. She was living in a palace, ruling her subjects in style.

For her kingdom was situated on caravan routes. *Two* of them. Camel caravans tracked up and down the desert—right *through* her territory. And ships tacked up and down the Red Sea—right past it. Her kingdom was like a tollgate! They all had to stop there. Camels had to be watered, people had to rest and get fresh supplies, ships had to wait for favorable winds.

And they were loaded! The camels were loaded and the ships were loaded—with gold and silver and ivory and all kinds of spices and precious stones and choice garments and carpets and rare woods—

And the people of Sheba were traders.

So you can see that between the trading they did and the tribute[1] the caravans and ships had to pay, the little kingdom was very rich. And so was the queen.

Now, gold and silver and jewels and merchandise were not the only things that traveled on the caravans and ships.

News traveled too. And gossip.

Yes, from all the people who came through, the queen could get a pretty good idea of what was going on in the world. Like which country was rich, which king was a nobody and which king was in *Who's Who*.

She was used to wild tales. Some of the stories that were told by the sailors and the caravan crews were really out of sight. But the stories told about this king up north called SOLOMON were the wildest ones of all.

He was the richest king in the world, they said.

1. That's a fancy name for tax.

He had built a Temple and several palaces that were beyond belief in magnificence and beauty.

He imported apes and peacocks to play in his gardens.

He had a huge ivory throne overlaid with pure gold. It had six steps with golden lions on either side—twelve lions in all.

All his cups and dishes were solid gold.

He even had gold armor and shields.

And his chariots were so many that he had special cities just to keep them in.

He was richer than all the kings of the earth—

And wiser. (Ah! *That* was what made the queen prick up her ears.)

They sang his songs. And they quoted his proverbs—

"If you want wisdom it will be given you, and knowledge of God himself. . . ."

"For the Lord grants wisdom! His every word is a treasure of knowledge and understanding."

"In everything you do, put God first, and he will direct you and crown your efforts with success."

"Wisdom gives: A long, good life—riches—honor—pleasure—and peace."

"The Lord's wisdom founded the earth. . . ."

And there was more. There was no end to the tales of Solomon's skill in finding hidden truth, and solving riddles, and of his wisdom.

She could see with her own eyes by the magnificence of his ships and caravans that he was rich. But could he really be *that* rich? And the tales of his doings were really impressive. But could he be *that* wise? Could *anybody?*

She had to see for herself.

And that's how it happened that the Queen of Sheba got ready a great caravan loaded with samples of all the goodies of her country. And trekked a thousand miles up that desert trade route to Jerusalem, to see the wisest man on all the earth.

Phew!

What a long tiresome way to go see something for yourself! And what did she find out?

Well, when she got to Jerusalem, it was not as she had expected.

It was so much *more*, so much *better*, so much *above and beyond* what she'd expected, that it left her goggle-eyed!

She went to splendid banquets and parties and sightseeing trips.

She saw the servants and the soldiers and the charioteers and the cupbearers and the wonderful foods on the king's table, and the splendid uniforms—

She talked with Solomon about affairs of state and trade agreements and riddles and deep problems, and he came up with the right answers to all her questions—there was nothing that he could not explain to her.

She saw the Temple and watched the sacrifices and heard him give all the glory to God—

Ah! Yes. God was everywhere. In the Temple. In the sacrifices. In this wise king's thinking. Everywhere.

For the wisdom this great king had—was the wisdom of God.

It was all so overwhelming that the Bible says there was no more spirit in her![2]

She told Solomon so, before she left. "Everything I heard is true," she said, "and more so! In fact, they did not tell me *half* of it!"

And she had her caravan unloaded and gave the king over three million dollars in gold, and a *huge* amount of jewels and spices. It was the greatest single gift he had ever received.

And then she went back to her country. But not with an empty caravan. It was loaded! For he gave her all the gifts he had planned *plus* everything she had asked for during her visit!

2. It took the wind out of her sails!

138

She went to see for herself. And she found much more than she'd expected. But the greatest thing she discovered was that God was the cause of it all. "Blessed be the Lord your God," she said to Solomon when she left. "How the Lord must love Israel!"

Yes, indeed.

You'd Like to See Some of Those Things for Yourself?

Well, you can. And you don't have to trek a thousand miles on a camel through the desert, either. You can just trek across the room, to that shelf, blow the dust off your Bible, open it—and read.

You'll find someone who is *greater than Solomon.*

Jesus, the Son of God.

He said so Himself.

"The Queen of Sheba went on a long, hard journey to listen to the wisdom of Solomon," He said, "but one far greater than Solomon is right here."[3]

He meant Himself!

And why was He "right here"? Why did He come? Why did God send Him?

Why, to be your Saviour!

"I have come to seek and to save those who are lost," He said.[4]

"But you must keep on believing the things you have been taught," the Bible tells us. "You know they are true for you know you can trust those of us who have taught you. You know how, when you were a small child, you were taught the holy Scriptures; and it is these that make you *wise* to accept God's salvation by trusting in Christ Jesus."[5]

You can see for yourself.

It's easy!

3. See Matthew 12:42 and Luke 11:31.
4. See Luke 19:10.
5. Second Timothy 3:14,15 (*TLB*).

You Want to Be Wise?

"Wisdom is the principal thing; therefore get wisdom: and with all thy getting, get understanding."[6]

Solomon said that.

"How can a man be wise? The only way to begin is by reverence for God."[7]

David said that.

You want to be wise?

It's the greatest wish you could ever have.

Believe on Jesus. Invite Him into your heart. And make that wish *today*.

"How the Lord must love Israel!" the Queen of Sheba said.

And how the Lord must love *you!*

Yes, indeed.

6. Proverbs 4:7 (*KJV*).
7. Psalm 111:10 (*TLB*).